Praise for *Are There Closets in Heaven?*

"I highly recommend t
pecially those who thin
tween their child and tl
many families who fol
disown their own child
Carol and Robert go t
struggles against a tradi
Such a heartwarming s

    —*Alfred Bertke, L*
    who supports hi

"Bob and Carol share
derstanding, compass
will serve as a map fo
the process of 'comin
those who are struggli
family will react to th
to parents who wonde

    —*Thomas B. Ho*
    Matthew Shep

"Poignant, personal,
story of one family's
vited into the vulnerable human perspective of the social struggles facing LGBT people and their families."

    —*Deb LeMay, Catholic Rainbow Parents*

"Bravo to the Curoe family, and especially to Bob and Carol, who together have written their story! This is a must-read for parents and families who are also struggling with these very personal feelings."

—Bill and Nancy Ross, parents of a gay son,
President of PFLAG, Dubuque, Iowa

"Gay and lesbian families are as diverse as their heterosexual counterparts. Read one family's powerful story beginning in their Iowan, Catholic roots through a journey of love and courage that demonstrates what unconditional love truly means."

—Laura Smidzik, Executive Director,
Rainbow Families

Are There Closets in Heaven?

A Catholic Father and Lesbian Daughter Share Their Story

C

SYREN BOOK COMPANY

MINNEAPOLIS

Published by
Syren Book Company
5120 Cedar Lake Road
Minneapolis, MN 55416
763-398-0030
www.syrenbooks.com

Printed in the United States of America on acid-free paper

ISBN 978-0-929636-79-5

LCCN 2007929924

Cover design by Kyle G. Hunter
Interior text design by Wendy Holdman
Edited by Mary Byers

To order additional copies of this book please go to
www.itascabooks.com

This book is dedicated to . . .

My life partner, Susan Langlee,
without whose love I would be lost

Patrick and Jonathan,
for showing me the true joy in life

Mom and Dad,
for teaching me all of life's really important lessons

Carol

My wife of fifty-two and a half years, Joyce Curoe. Joyce passed away suddenly on May 22, 2007, at home. In the beginning of writing this book, she was reluctant to support the project because she wasn't sure that we should go public with the personal moments of our lives. She never tried to stop us, however, and in the end became a very strong supporter. I dedicate this book to Joyce for her love of us and her acceptance that this story needs to be told to help other families overcome prejudice and accept their gay children.

Robert

Contents

Acknowledgments

We extend special thanks to . . .

Mike, Joann, Kevin, Patty, and Tim, children and siblings, for their loving support and gentle permission to let us tell our story

Mike and Tim, sons and brothers, for their careful reading of the manuscript and keeping us honest

Nathan, grandson and nephew, for letting us include his college application essay

Dani, Laura, Lisa, and Terryl, friends who listened to "book talk" for years and always acted interested

PART I

The Letter

Chapter One

Tuesday, September 18, 1990. I recall every detail of that fall day, although I can't claim I had any special awareness of what was on the horizon before I read the letter. I didn't sense what was coming as I did when I saw the strange light that preceded the Category 4 tornado that ripped through a few miles from us earlier in the spring. I didn't feel the heaviness and electricity of the air before a storm. I'm a farmer. I'm from Iowa. I don't need to see darkening clouds to know there is trouble coming and I must get home.

But I had no such intuition that day of how my life was about to change.

When fall arrives, I am out of bed at 5:30 A.M., down the road, and in the fields or feeding the animals by 6:00 A.M. That day, the sun shone bright and I raked hay all morning. The only sound was that of the tractor as I moved through the fields. The hay will be bundled into huge round bales, each weighing 1,200–1,500 pounds. It's been a long time since stacks or square bales have been seen in the fields of eastern Iowa. The big equipment that is needed to form and lift those large round bales can roll in a field, trapping a farmer underneath, or pull in a hand or an arm as easily as hoist a ton of hay. Farming is a profession for those who are alert, and not for the faint of heart.

As I ride the tractor through the fields, it is only when I am on top of the hills that I can see a few farmhouses, maybe half a mile away. Trees surround these houses and barns, or grow along the banks of a meandering creek. The pine tree windbreaks line up alongside the homes, fending off the snow, rain, or wind before the weather assaults the house. In autumn the trees in Iowa blaze with color, and September brings the first signs of yellow and orange in willow, cottonwood, black walnut, green ash, box elder, elm, hackberry, and birch trees. In Dubuque County, our county, the main fall colors are the ripening bright yellow soybeans and the corn turning brown. The unpracticed eye might think the corn is dead at this stage, but the shades of brown merely signal that the corn is maturing, ready to be harvested.

That day, I came home for lunch at noon and Joyce met me at the door. I was introduced to her almost forty years before at a dance in Cascade, a town only twelve miles from where we live now. I married her less than a year later, and since then we've been through family and community upheavals of every kind. She had a look on her face that fall day I had never seen before. Her eyes were red from crying and her mouth was grim. It had to be devastating news. I assumed a sudden death in the family.

"Read this," she said, pointing to a letter on the table. I prepared myself for the worst, while Joyce lowered her gaze and stared straight at the floor. I read quickly, my eyes darting across the page, wanting to get to the tragic news as soon as possible. I could digest the details later.

September 13, 1990

Dear Mom and Dad,

Writing this letter is probably one of the most difficult things I've had to do. I've never done anything to hurt you, and never would. But I know what I'm going to tell you will cause both of you some pain; and I wish I could avoid it.

Maybe it won't come as a complete surprise, but it probably will be a shock even if you suspected it.

Mom and Dad, I'm gay. I always have been and I always will be. I am in a very committed relationship with Susan and have been for over three years. I love her very much and am very happy.

If I could make this easier for you, I would. I've even thought of not telling you at all. But you are both such a special part of my life that I cannot keep such an important aspect of my life from you. It's been very difficult keeping so much from you over the past three-plus years. Although I knew I couldn't tell you until I was ready, I still felt as if I was living a lie.

Being gay is not something that happens overnight or as a response to any particular relationship. I was gay long before any dating. My determination to make earlier relationships work was more of an attempt to just make it work because that's what I was "supposed" to do. It was part of the picture I had of myself at the time.

I didn't choose to be gay anymore than someone chooses to be left-handed. I do believe, however, that we still make certain choices in our lives—that's one belief which has gotten me as far as I am today. A gay person cannot choose how he/she feels, but they can choose how they are going to live their life. There are a lot of homosexuals who choose to deny their true feelings and live a "straight" life rather than deal with upsetting family and close friends or even risk the possibility of losing them. For some, this works and they are able to live happy fulfilled lives. For others, they are never truly happy without accepting themselves for who and what they really are.

I've been through a long and somewhat difficult process of self-acceptance to get to where I am now. But I am gay and I can accept what that means to me. Susan and I love each other very much. We have a beautiful home, good jobs, and a lot of good friends. We are both living very healthy, happy and productive lives which is what so many people strive for in life. Some are never lucky enough to find it. The biggest thing missing in our lives has been the support of our families.

I decided to tell you in a letter to give you a chance to gather your emotions before responding or reacting to the news I've just shared with you. Secondly, there are so many things I wanted to tell you that I wasn't sure I would be able to in person.

As for timing, last Christmas, Susan and I decided that we wouldn't spend holidays apart anymore. It was too difficult to be together with family and have such an important member missing. Since you are planning to spend Christmas with us in Phoenix, I want to give you enough time to decide if you still want to come. If you're not ready yet, I can understand and accept that.

I realize this is not an issue that one accepts overnight, especially about their daughter. I understand the kind of time it may take to work through this, and realize that I've had a lot more time to accept this than you have. There's a grieving process one has to go through for the loss of what you pictured for me as my future, and replacing it with a new image, and one that right now is a pretty foreign concept; that of a gay person living a happy and productive life with her partner. I want to help you as much as I can in this process, and I'll give you as much time as it takes. But whenever you want to talk about it, I do too.

I want to tell you what I hope we will all work towards. I have no expectations of how long it will take because it is an ongoing process. But I do believe in my family. I know we have all felt very blessed and fortunate to be part of our family. We've been a tremendous support for one another, and I hope this continues. I've seen other families of gay friends accept them and their partners openly, and yet I still haven't seen one family with the same commitment and bonds that we have.

I hope that eventually you will be able to accept

this, and try your best to understand it. I'll never expect anyone to fully understand. I'm still working on that myself. But I hope you will be able to accept Susan and me and just keep working on trying to understand. I'd like you to take an active interest in mine and Susan's life, to read what you can, ask questions, talk to each other, and possibly attend support groups. You'll find there really are a lot of other parents going through exactly what you are.

I want to be able to talk openly about my life in the same way that all my siblings share their lives. I hope someday Susan will be welcomed into our family just as we have welcomed all in-laws. I hope you can love me and Susan just as you did ten minutes ago before you read this letter. We're exactly the same people we were then. I know this must sound like a lot to ask right now, but there is no time frame attached.

I'll support you in any way I can, and I hope you can ask me for anything you need—even if it's just time. I'm sending this to everyone in the family so you have them to turn to for support also. Patty and Joann have known for a while so they should be good support.

I know you both want more than anything for me to be happy, and what I want most is for you to know that I am. Please remember that. I won't call to see if you received this. When you're ready I'll hear from you.

I love you both very, very much.
Carol

I had the same feeling of dread as when Pearl Harbor was bombed, JFK was shot, President Roosevelt died, the atomic bomb dropped on Hiroshima.

My daughter is gay.

PART II

Packing for the Trip

Chapter Two

My life with Dad is a series of vignettes that have two main themes: my striving for his attention and his desire to make me strong, to live up to my greatest potential. As early as I can remember, I yearned to get more of Dad's attention. Maybe it was because I was one of six children, or maybe it was because Dad worked a lot and exactly what he did was elusive to me. Elusive, not because I didn't "know" what happens on a farm, but mysterious because as a girl I had my own role on the farm and it didn't intersect with Dad's and my brothers' roles. Farms are about endless work, and it seems to happen best if everyone has their role and follows it. The three sisters were inside the house, putting the meals on for the men, washing dishes, cleaning, and doing the laundry. The three brothers were outside with Dad, feeding the livestock, breaking horses, and driving tractors, or so it seemed. My brothers say they did laundry, too, but I don't think so.

We lived in a brick rambler. For most of my childhood, the house had three bedrooms and one bathroom for five kids and both parents. When Tim, the sixth child was born, his crib was squeezed into the small room

Patty and I already shared. We were only six and seven years old, but we took care of the night feedings and changed diapers. We learned to care for others by caring for each other. There was always yardwork—it took four hours to mow. All of our barns are on the same side of the road as the house. One year my dad decided to paint them brown—a break from the tradition of the red barn that every other farmer in Iowa seems to have on his property. The road in front was gravel until I was in high school. When a car drove by, the dust cloud rose up and rolled in through the windows, coating the furniture with a light brown film. Just as the dust intruded on us night and day, my mother cleaned relentlessly. She dusted and vacuumed and yelled at us to keep the windows closed.

Rolling hills surrounded the farm. To the south the hill was so high, even climbing a tree didn't work—you had to walk to the hilltop to see the community beyond our farm.

A pine tree grove to the west of the house served as a windbreak. Almost everyone had a windbreak—the weather on the Iowa grasslands can be brutal in the winter and fierce during spring and summer storms. If you've traveled through the American Midwest, you know that weather is a favorite topic of conversation. *What about that thunderstorm last night? Took the elm tree down at the McClures'. Missed the house by inches. Did you see the Flannerys' car? Tornado drove a metal pole straight through the hood. School closings. Freezing rain advisory.*

White-out conditions. Power line damage due to ice storms. These labels conjure up specific days and nights out on the farm when we ran for shelter, headed to the barn to check the animals, or cheered because we wouldn't be getting on the bus to school. Weather scares you in the country, but it also makes you feel invincible every time you make it through another season when the weather was the worst it's been in decades.

In the mornings, we girls always said good-bye to Dad from the top of the stairs. He dressed downstairs and went directly outside to start work. The house was Mom's domain, just like the barns and the fields were his. He was not allowed to come upstairs with his work clothes or boots. Mom was adamant about trying to keep the farm smells out of the house, a never-ending task with six kids and a husband working the land and raising animals for food and income.

One morning after breakfast, when I was seven years old, I heard Dad head downstairs to put on his coveralls and boots. This was a special day. I had been excused from doing the breakfast dishes because I was going to help Dad with the chores. I frantically tried to get my coat and boots on quickly enough to meet Dad outside. I had to be ready when he was or he would just head out to the barns to get the chores done without me. I could hear the crackle of fat and then smell the bacon, eggs and coffee as I threw on my pants and shirt. Dad was fast, hurrying through his breakfast and putting on his jacket. I heard the dull thud of his boots hit the kitchen floor. I was losing ground. I called downstairs, "Dad, help me put on my boots!" I could have asked Mom to help, but that would not detain Dad. I needed to hold him back or I was going to be left behind. If I wasn't there by the time he was on the porch steps, I would spend the day in the house instead of helping out on the farm. I heard the basement door slam as he left the house. I was only seconds behind.

I ran after Dad through the cattle yard, the early morning warm smells of manure filling the air. I watched him fill the large hanging bucket with cattle feed. I jumped right in, ready to push the hanging bucket out along the bunkers, even though it was too heavy for me to push alone. He reached over and put his gloved hands above mine, pushing the bucket along. There wasn't much conversation between us. That wasn't the point. I was just happy to be alone with Dad.

I was six when Dad chose me to help break Campion, our new colt. Campion was fiery, high-spirited, and had broken free from more than one of us kids. He galloped across the fields while we ran behind calling for help from the adults. I don't know why he chose me, but I never turned down a chance to work with Dad. Breaking Campion, held in high regard by the family, was a golden opportunity to receive the hard-to-earn attention and recognition I craved. Breaking a horse was a straightforward job. Dad put the saddle on Campion and helped me mount. All I had to do was hang on while he led me around with our other horse as a guide. I was sure I could hang on tight enough to the saddle horn so that I wouldn't fall off and get stepped on or kicked. I had more than respect for these beasts. I was afraid of horses, but I kept that to myself. Dad loved horses, trail rides, driving the horse and buggy in summer and the horse and sleigh in the deep winter snows, and I wasn't going to appear to be weak or let him down by telling him my fears.

We circled the field. I was riding high and happy with Dad in front of me on the other horse. Suddenly, a roar off to the side signaled a motorcycle tearing down the gravel road, scattering gravel and dust. Campion tensed, spooked, and reared up. The reins were jerked out of Dad's hand. I lost my hold on that little saddle horn. Did I fly through the air? Go hurtling over Campion's head? Some days I remember it like that; other days, my memory tells me I fell over backwards and landed with a hard thump on my back. It knocked the wind out of me and filled me with instant terror. Dad says I merely fell to the side, onto the ground, which was soft enough since it was spring. No matter how I landed—on my head, on my butt, on the soft ground or the hard ground—I know adrenaline raced in my veins. I can feel that still. I had been doing a traditional man's job out there—I had gotten to do it. But running side by side with the adrenaline and pride was fear.

It's over, I thought. Dad helped me back onto my feet and gave me a quick check to make sure I was all right. "I don't have any broken bones. I'm alive."

I was quivering, trying to look nonchalant as if my

body didn't feel bruised and banged up. We would go back to the house now. I would sit at the kitchen table and drink hot chocolate while my mother, brothers, and sisters insisted I tell the story about Campion over and over. They would want to know exactly what happened and shake their heads in amazement at my courage. I would be the hero—the girl who survived breaking Campion.

I looked over at Dad. He was holding Campion steady, waiting for me to get back on. "I'm not having you develop a lifelong fear of horses," he said.

"But Dad," rang loudly in my head as he lifted my protesting body onto Campion's back. "I was scared before we even started today. Now I'm terrified." I didn't say anything, though. He took the reins in his hand and we kept on riding.

Attention and approval from Dad were only part of my agenda. I wanted the same from my brother Kevin, who was three and a half years older than me, almost as much as I wanted it from Dad. If Kevin and I were getting along, it meant that we were probably getting in trouble together. We threw rocks at cars passing by after church and then sped into the house, hiding in the bathroom or behind furniture, claiming safe haven. One day a driver didn't let us get away with that. He backed up, jumped out, and came right to the door to confront the parents of the juvenile delinquents who had pelted his car. We cowered behind the curtains until we were pulled out to apologize by our parents.

Kevin and I shared a special love for fire. I was entranced by the danger of matches and staring into the blue edge that enclosed the glowing flames. He was fearless, eager to teach me all about matches and fire, and I was eager to impress him with my quick learning ability. I was five when we went into the machine shed, closed the door, and hid in the shadow of the riding lawn mower.

We took matches out of the red-and-blue box with the strutting rooster on the top and, one at a time, struck them against the sandpapery strip. We waited just long enough to see the flame shoot up and burn halfway to our fingers before blowing them out. They didn't always get blown out. I was nervous, afraid of burning my fingers, and sometimes threw a still-lit match on the shed floor. Those we stomped, kicking dirt over the tiny yellow flames before they turned into a blaze. It wasn't long until I gained the confidence to repeatedly light the matches on my own. When I no longer needed Kevin, the fascination evaporated and we both quickly lost interest.

We were running out of the shed just as Mom's voice reached us, calling everyone to get ready for Saturday evening Mass. I climbed into the tub with my younger sister Patty, while our older sister Joann knelt beside. Joann massaged shampoo into our hair, sudsing and then pouring the pitcher of water over our heads. Through the squeals and dowsing, we all heard the high-pitched scream of the sirens. A siren on the gravel country road was a rare occurrence. If you heard one, it was time for the family to jump in the car and chase it down to see what was happening and whether you could help. If you didn't do that, you could pick up the phone and just listen in as all of your neighbors on the party line talked back and forth, trading theories on the destination of the fire truck or ambulance that had sped down the road. That day, the sirens seemed to go past our house, toward the next farm. Maybe an elderly neighbor had had a heart attack. Maybe someone's hand got caught in the mower. Maybe a small brushfire along the road had spiraled out of control. A few minutes later, Dad squeezed his way into the narrow bathroom. I can see his jeans and light blue denim work shirt tucked into his pants—the farm uniform of choice. His face was red and his mouth was an angry straight line. He didn't waste any time going after Patty or Joann. He had no words and no doubt about my guilty status. Dad grabbed me by the arm and yanked me straight out of the tub, all the while spanking me across my wet, bare bottom. The water amplified both the sting and the *slap, slap* sound as he held me with his other hand.

It only took me a moment to figure out that our house, and more specifically the machine shed, had been the real destination of the fire trucks. I suspected Kevin had squealed on me, offered me up as a sacrifice, but even if Dad had guessed, I would never have tried to deny it. In our house, guilty or not, the worst thing you could do was lie about an offense.

Disappointing Dad was worse than any physical punishment he could have delivered.

In a pile of photos that keeps resurfacing over the years, moved from drawer to drawer, always waiting to be filed chronologically or by location somewhere in a neat scrapbook, there is a photo of Dad and me holding a balsa wood model bridge when I was in ninth grade. Dad had seen an announcement in the local paper about a bridge-building contest at the University of Wisconsin at Platteville and encouraged me to enter. The challenge: design a bridge using balsa wood and see how much weight it would hold before breaking. He pointed out that few girls would enter this competition. It would be a chance for me to stand out.

This project was different from many school assignments. My friends often appeared at school with projects with which parents had obviously helped, but not us. Mom and Dad believed in letting us do our own schoolwork. The bridge-building contest, however, somehow seemed different. Dad and I purchased the prescribed materials together, designed it on paper, and then took turns holding the balsa wood while the other did the gluing. We spent hours hunkered over the dining room table. He was immersed in the project and helped me every step of the way. I didn't complain. I tired of our bridge long before Dad did, but I stayed with it anyway. I traveled to the contest in a nearby city with a group from school to exhibit the masterpiece. Dad had work to do on the farm, and, after all, it was supposed to be my project, not his. At the judging, a boy from our town had used materials that weren't allowed. He lost outright. I was nervous when the load went on. They piled on a bit at a time to see how much it would hold. Our bridge swayed to the side under the weight, twisted and eventually collapsed. We didn't win anything, but we didn't embarrass ourselves either.

Three years after the bridge-building experiment, Dad and I sat at the dining room table again, poring over the interest inventories I had filled out with the school guidance counselor. I had no idea what I wanted to be when I grew up, an area of "indecision" I've carried with me throughout my entire life. My sister Patty loved to take care of people and always knew she would be a nurse. My sister Joann knew all along she would be a teacher. She taught every kid she ever babysat and loved it from the beginning.

Dad and I tried to make a life plan for me, tried to make sense out of the jagged graphs that purported to demonstrate my strengths and weaknesses. There were three strong suits—architecture, engineering, and teaching. Teaching fit. There were many teachers in our family, and Dad had great respect for them. Besides Joann, I can name several without even thinking: Mom's sister-in-law, Mom's sisters Janice, Pat, and Kathy, Kathy's husband, Dad's two sisters who were nuns, and at least three great-aunts.

I leaned toward teaching. It was familiar and something I knew I could do well. Dad's message to me: "Are you sure?" ran counter to my own intuition.

Dad zeroed in on engineering. The bridge-building competition had come back to haunt me. Engineering? I wasn't even sure what engineering was. He tried to persuade me to choose this field and had all the talking points down. I was an excellent student. I had a detail-oriented mind. I was tough, not easily daunted by a challenge. There weren't very many female engineers—the field was wide open for women to enter and advance. It all made sense. Dad, more than anyone, knew I was a good student, particularly in math and science. He was the one who'd spent countless hours coaching and tutoring me through high school math.

I didn't have the debate points down to counter his well-thought-out and enthusiastic presentation. In the absence of a compelling desire of my own for any one career field, I decided Dad's rationale for engineering was as good as any reason I had for another choice. I couldn't convince him, or myself, that teaching made more sense than engineering. He said if he were starting over himself, he would be an engineer. For me, the girl, now grown into a young woman who loved her dad, this was a factor in choosing engineering.

I applied to universities and played up the doomed bridge project as an example of my dedicated interest in this field. I didn't know what type of engineering I should choose. I finally decided on civil engineering because it seemed to be the most people-oriented field. I would be working with teams of people building structures for people to use. There were no role models. I had never met a civil engineer, let alone a female engineer.

Over the years, I've met scores of women with virtually the same story—someone who encouraged them, or pushed them, depending on who's telling the story, to become an engineer, for all of the same reasons Dad had: "You're a woman, you're good in math and science; you should go into engineering."

I graduated from high school as salutatorian of my class. The local newspaper printed the list of senior year honor roll students at Beckman High School, the Catholic high school I attended. I wasn't on it. Our neighbors and friends assumed the local newspaper had made a mistake. My family knew my name wasn't included because I didn't care about grades those last months. They'd watched me move on socially and emotionally; I was ready to be out of high school and acted as if I already was.

Life as I knew it was coming to an end. I was self-centered and needed to spend as much time with my friends as possible. The weeks flew by, as I ignored parental curfews, skipped over details for college, and dismissed family obligations that would have been high on my list a few months before. Our group of friends did something different every night. I buzzed in and out of the house with a wave of the hand and a sketchy report on what I had been doing and where I was going. I was eighteen.

I was independent. I spent almost no time getting ready for my freshman year at Marquette University.

The night before leaving for Marquette, I should have been home packing. Instead, I went out with friends for one last party. We got everything together for a picnic and drove into Wisconsin, fifty miles away, for the evening. In Wisconsin the drinking age was only eighteen, and it was the place to go for Iowa kids who wanted to party. Our friends piled into two cars. My boyfriend, Terry, drove a souped-up red Chevy Nova. I was driving my parents' brand-new, two-tone brown Oldsmobile Delta 88. I was cool—it was my farewell party and I was the center of attention.

Several hours later, we cruised back into Iowa slightly tipsy on beer, my friends hanging out the car windows feeling the heat of summer still rising off the fields. When we got near Dyersville, we took a gravel road detour. Terry in the red Nova was the competition. I gunned the Olds, pushing the pedal to the floor. The Nova quickly pulled ahead. My friends screamed along with me as we maneuvered to catch up, flying through the gravel, which sprayed out in every direction. We were making headway, bearing down on the Nova, until we roared into a ninety-degree bend in the road going fifty-five. The Olds fishtailed, whipping back and forth in the road. We were tossed from side to side, still shrieking with excitement, tempered by an undercurrent of fear. I gripped the steering wheel, trying to control the erratic spin. I had years of training in how to correct a slide on ice during Iowan winters—steer into the direction of the slide, don't work against it. That strategy didn't work on the country road. Over what seemed like hours, we careened sideways through the loose gravel into a steep ditch and rolled twice through a cornfield. The Olds tore out a hundred yards of fence and landed back on the wheels with a sickening thump.

We forced open the bashed-in doors and extricated ourselves from the car, stunned. Inspecting each other, we saw only minor scratches and bruises, and shattered glass glinted in our hair and stuck to our clothes. No broken necks or legs. No bloody eyes or missing teeth. The car wasn't so lucky. The top and hood were caved in, leaving hollows in the metal like a smashed egg carton. The new brown paint my Dad liked so much was now a network of deep gouges.

Minutes later, our friends in the red Nova came back down the road looking for us. They had turned around immediately when we didn't show up in town. We spent the next thirty minutes discussing what our "story" was going to be. We had to be on the same page before we talked to our parents. Everyone had a different angle about where we had been, what we had been doing, how the car crashed, grappling for a version that would minimize parental wrath and stave off possible questioning from the police.

I was never an effective liar, and I knew this was too big to even try. "I don't think I can pull off lying," I told my friends. "But I can probably convince my parents to maintain your story, if that's what you want."

We all climbed into the red Nova for the drive to my friend's home. I prepared myself along the way for Dad's anger and his disappointment that his daughter was so foolish as to risk property and many lives. At my friend's house, I called Dad. I steeled myself for rage to come flying back at me through the phone. He never erupted, scolded, or chastised. He was concerned about two things: our safety and how to haul the car out of the farmer's field. That night, Dad made all the arrangements with the towing company and handled the details with the insurance company, allowing me to slip to the side and spend the rest of the night distractedly getting ready for school.

The next morning, I took a break from packing and went to Dad's office.

"You're lucky you weren't hurt or someone wasn't killed," he said. He didn't need to say it out loud—the whole family had been saying it all night.

"How fast were you going?" he asked.

"About fifty or fifty-five miles per hour," I ventured. I could hardly hear my own voice. I learned to drive out there in the country, on that same gravel road. Only a fool or a city person would drive on that loose gravel faster than thirty miles per hour.

"I didn't expect you to tell me the truth on that point," he said, laughing at my chagrined face. "Of course, I knew you were speeding way beyond the limit. That accident couldn't have happened any other way."

Then the conversation took a serious slant. Dad felt the accident was his fault.

"I should have dealt with your behavior this summer." Dad began to cry. "I knew you were staying out later and later every night. I just hoped you would stay safe until you left for college."

He blamed himself for my crazy behavior. That was the toughest punishment I could have received. Yelling, anger, or restrictions would all have been easier to take. I hated letting him down. I wanted to take it all back. I wanted him to be proud of me again: the class salutatorian, sports team captain, and student council member, not the wild daughter who almost killed herself and her friends in a car speeding down a gravel road on the last night of summer.

I made it to Marquette and survived freshman orientation. I was a small-town girl, but in some ways my first year away from home was an extension of my summer. Every night there was a round of social activities and I stayed out late, talking to new friends and exploring the campus neighborhood with hundreds of other students. I was game for anything. One evening a hypnotist did a presentation. I was one of the students in the audience who was hypnotized. It happened easily and I fell into a deep dreamlike zone. The hypnotist kept insisting that I come up on the stage with the other hypnotized students, but I refused—though it didn't keep me from following his suggestions in my front row seat! I chalked it up later to being very tired and therefore susceptible.

I signed up to try out for the volleyball team. I hadn't planned to do that and had no expectations of making the team. I simply wanted to have a good time—to have a chance to play with college-level players. The day after tryouts, I found the list posted on the wall. I had made the varsity team for a Division One program. I was so excited I couldn't sit still, and the first thing I did was phone Mom and Dad. The pride in their voices began to wash away my guilt over disappointing them during the summer.

Every Wednesday in college, I could expect a letter from Dad. There were always at least three siblings in college at the same time, and Dad wrote one letter and used carbon paper to make the other copies. He rotated who received the original each week. Sometimes, the letter was hard to read because it was my turn to receive the last carbon copy, but it didn't matter. It was mail from my family. Before e-mail, a letter in your mailbox was a big deal. Dad told us what he and Mom were doing, about the animals and the work on the farm, a few details here and there about the neighbors. All the stories that mean little to the outside world, but everything to us who had moved away.

Valentine's Day that freshman year rolled around, and many of my friends had dates for parties and dinners. Not me. Valentine's Day without a date wasn't an anomaly in my life. I had never been much of a dater. I had a list of possible reasons running in my mind: I was in sports. I strayed from my ideal weight. I just wasn't very attractive. In hindsight, I realize it was because I hadn't figured out yet whom I should be dating. The dorm and the campus were decorated with all of the pink and red hearts and crepe paper that hopeful romantics put up everywhere. People sold roses in the student union and the stores were filled with frilly and sappy greeting cards for your boyfriend or girlfriend.

I came back from classes that day and found a dozen roses for me at the front desk of the dorm. The receptionist and my friends oohed and aahed over the beautiful flowers, thinking I had a sweetheart I hadn't mentioned and guessing at who it might be. I kept a sly smile on my face. I wasn't giving out any information about my secret admirer. They didn't need to know the red roses were from my father. Roses on Valentine's Day arrived as an annual event. I looked forward to them because they connected me to Dad and gave me a cover in terms of my romantic life I didn't even know I needed.

Dad stopped this tradition when we were all out of school, which made me sad. "Now most of you have spouses and boyfriends who can take over this task," he forewarned us. "It won't be happening anymore." I was one of the siblings who was going to have to buy my own roses if they were going to arrive on my Valentine's Day doorstep.

Chapter Three

Carol, out of all six children, was the one child I had to
be very careful with what I said, because she would do
what I suggested. She'd come into my office and take a
chair and ask for my advice. And she would listen. The
other kids—they might or might not listen.

She was not what you'd call an easy baby or an easy
child. She was always getting into something. She was
running. She was knocking a brother or sister down,
brushing past a table and sending a book or plate flying to the floor. She was an independent thinker, starting way back when she was a child. Joyce says Carol and
I are both stubborn. I say I am more determined than
stubborn.

Carol didn't take "no" well at all. She questioned the
teachers, challenging anything that didn't make sense to
her. Some of the teachers admired it, but many didn't
like it at all. They had to really know what they were
teaching because she would be right there asking questions and pinning them down. She certainly wasn't a
teacher's pet with that approach.

Early in life Carol displayed leadership in terms of
organizing her friends in games and an uncanny ability

to motivate herself. A few days before she was to start school she broke her leg in a playground accident. I was at the hospital with her.

"You can go home as soon as you learn to use the crutches," the doctor said to Carol. She had just been fitted for them, shown how to use them, and was gamely trying them out while we both watched. I felt sorry for this little girl who would be spending days getting used to wooden crutches under her armpits, keeping her from running and playing with her friends, getting her first school days off to a halting start.

I was at the nurse's station a few minutes later and there was a laugh and a series of soft thumps behind me in the hall. It was Carol, the crutches under her arms, a big smile on her face.

"Can I go home now?" she shouted in our direction. "I'm ready."

Carol was not only self-motivated, she was mischievous, especially when she got together with her older brother, Kevin. I was sitting on the porch with Joyce, at the end of a long day working in the fields. As we talked, we both commented on the large amount of dust blowing across the yard. It lifted up into the air and wisped across the lawn, gradually thickening until it began to obscure the barns and the shade trees. We couldn't figure out where it could be coming from. Suddenly we both realized it wasn't dust at all, it was smoke. The machine shed was on fire. I ran to the shed while Joyce called the fire department. I swatted at the fire with burlap bags and was lucky to get it under control before it really took off and destroyed everything on our property.

I was out and out mad. Fires don't start by themselves. I'm not sure how I knew it was Carol—I just knew. All of the kids had been out playing in the yard, and Carol and Kevin disappeared for a bit. Maybe that was the clue. But there really wasn't any doubt in my mind. They could have been badly hurt and could have destroyed the farm, all with that one incident. I ran up to the bathroom where the girls were getting bathed and didn't think twice before I grabbed Carol out of the tub and smacked her on the behind. She didn't deny it. All of our kids knew that if they lied about what they had done, the punishment would be twice as bad. I never thought any of them would lie to me about anything.

Our kids were familiar with horses. We used them on the farm a lot—to herd cattle into the corral so they could be artificially inseminated. I didn't know until years later, when Carol was an adult, that she didn't like horses, that she had even been afraid of them. She never told me that. She was probably five or six at the time we went out together to break Campion, our favorite horse and a feisty one. Campion was only two years old and too small for an adult to ride. His mother was a small grade mare, bred to a purebred Arabian stallion. We had Campion for about thirty years. I thought the sun rose and set on that horse.

It doesn't matter how good the bloodline, there comes the time when you have to break a young horse, train him to accept a rider and follow your commands. None of the other kids in the family would have anything to do with breaking Campion—they had all witnessed his free spirit. Only Carol was willing, even though she hadn't ridden to any great degree.

It was a Sunday afternoon, a nice spring day, everything greening. We crossed from the house over to the field and saddled up Campion. It was going well until a motorcycle sped by and the colt, which was always skittish, reared. I don't remember Carol really being thrown, although that's what it felt like to her. It was more like she fell off backwards when the horse reared. I don't think she was even frightened. I was scared, of course, afraid she'd gotten hurt, but saw right away she hadn't. She was ready to quit, but I didn't give her the option. I think everyone knows the old adage about getting back on a horse that throws you—that kind of proverb works in most arenas in life, but in this case, it was literally the right thing to do.

We didn't just use horses on the farm. Sunday was for family trail rides sponsored by the local saddle clubs. It was a community event, sometimes fifty families and 150 horses. We'd start midmorning and ride all day. It wasn't a hard ride, the horses walked the trail. Running the horses was against the rules. Too many people for that. We'd have lunch along the way and get back about 6:00 in the evening. Everyone had to get back—we were all farm families and had to be home in time for chores.

Carol brought friends home from high school and

college to go on these family trail rides. They would arrive over the weekend, with suitcases filled with jeans and sneakers, interested in country life. They walked the property and hung out in the barns while Carol showed them life on the farm. On Sunday, we'd choose the horses for them that were easy to handle. None of that Campion stuff for inexperienced riders. We were lucky we didn't have a serious accident. For many of them, their experience with big animals had been limited to riding on a carousel at an amusement park.

Carol had lots of friends, both boys and girls. We were always interested in her male companions, and she brought home several boys, each of whom seemed like an excellent prospect for a boyfriend. One young man showed up in a neat, pressed suit. They were going out to dinner. We talked to him in the living room while Carol got ready. He was a nice boy, eager to make a good impression on us, telling us about his parents and his school interests. Carol walked into the room, ready to go out for the evening with this promising young man. She was dressed in jeans and a sweatshirt.

He looked dismayed. We were, too.

Never saw him again.

I don't believe I ever knew a woman who was an engineer. Twenty years ago, women were in the minority in all of those fields. Carol was an achiever—she could do anything she set her mind to, so even though there weren't many women engineers, I never doubted she could do it, and do it well. She had a mechanical mind. Even from the time she was a child she could tell what needed to be fixed if something broke down on the farm. She didn't necessarily know how to fix it, but she could analyze the problem and tell me what was wrong.

I know I led Carol into engineering, but it wasn't only her. I encouraged her younger brother to be an engineer, too, although, like Carol, he doesn't actively use his degree now. I thought engineering was such a versatile career—it could take Carol into so many fields. If she didn't like it, she could use her skills in many other areas. A lot of employers will look at an engineer and think, If they're smart enough to do calculus and everything that getting an engineering degree entails, then I can teach them to do anything I need at this job.

I read about a contest at the University of Wisconsin-Platteville for high school students and thought Carol should enter. It involved building a bridge out of balsa wood. They gave you the dimensions of the structure, and you couldn't use anything other than the specified materials. You could use less than what was in the packet but not more. One of Carol's classmates made his a few inches shorter and was disqualified in the final contest. We were more precise. We followed the rules exactly. While we worked on the bridge, we took a lot of pictures, proud of what we were creating. These photos turn up now and then, on the side of the refrigerator or at the bottom of a pile of family memories in a cardboard box.

The bridge didn't collapse when it was loaded with

the weight during the judging, but it leaned drastically sideways. Carol blamed me and I blamed her. We both learned something. I didn't actually go to the competition site—it was ninety minutes away and I needed to work. I really thought we would do better than that. I guess I missed out on a basic engineering lesson.

I did have a good head for business, however, and Carol shares that. I had no college; I only went to high school. I was a decent student and graduated with honors, but that wasn't a big deal. Growing up in my family there was never even a question of our future: you were either a farmer or a priest. If you were going to be a priest, you went to a Jesuit college. If you were going to be a farmer, you didn't need to go to college. The soil of the greater part of our state is a dark drift loam ranging from two to five feet deep and can host almost any type of crop, but corn and soybeans reign supreme. I have no regrets about being a farmer—it's fed and educated our family very well.

Carol really wanted to go to Notre Dame. Her brother Mike was at Notre Dame, and we thought she was a shoo-in with her high grades, letters in three sports, and multiple activities. But Notre Dame said they wouldn't accept her without a certain math class she hadn't taken. She didn't let that deter her. She got a tutor and studied all through Christmas vacation her senior year. When she took the tests, she fulfilled the requirement but was still placed on the waiting list.

Suddenly, she seemed to take a turn in her focus, and

the next weekend we went to Milwaukee to take a look at Marquette University. Marquette told her they would accept her on the spot. Notre Dame later came to its senses, but by then she had shifted her thoughts to Marquette.

Carol was lax those last weeks before summer ended after she graduated from high school. She was always independent, but those weeks especially I felt she needed time to be with her friends. We gave her a free rein to spend her time the way she wanted. We saw her coming and going, dressed for a concert or a barbeque, a gang of her friends arriving and driving off or her speeding away in our new Oldsmobile.

Maybe I should have seen it coming. It was after midnight, the night before Carol was to leave for college, when she called from a friend's home. Her voice was quaking. She had been in an accident, driving our brand-new car. The car had gone off the road, through a ditch, took out a fence, and was now stuck in a farmer's field. I insisted they go to the hospital, but her friend's mother was a nurse and got on the phone. She said the girls were only shaken up, scratched a little. No one was hurt.

I arranged with the tow truck to get it out of the field. I couldn't believe it when I saw the car all smashed in, the windshield broken, the doors jammed shut. It was totaled. Then I questioned the wisdom of them not going to the hospital. It was lucky they lived to tell the tale. There was never any question of fixing it—one look told you it was all over for that car. The farmer couldn't have been more agreeable. He was just glad it wasn't his own daughter.

I was furious at Carol, but actually I blamed myself. Joyce was angry with her, too. The drive to Milwaukee the next day was a tough one—it was very quiet in the car. No one had anything to say that could take away the events of the night before. The fact that our bright daughter with such a promising future could have been taken away in one foolish night was a somber cloud hanging in the air.

But then she was at Marquette and doing so well, the accident and the shock of it started to fade to the background. She went out for volleyball and made the team. Joyce and I were both proud of her for that. She did well in her classes, and she made friends. I'd say her transition to the next phase of her life went pretty smoothly.

I wrote to all of our kids at college every week, for all the years they were there. I'd write the letter over the weekend and they'd get it on Wednesday. It was mostly farm talk, nothing of great importance, I suppose, but they liked it anyway. I never put much value on those letters. There was no such thing as a copy machine in those days, let alone a computer and certainly not at home. So I wrote the letters and used carbon paper to make copies for the other kids. It was important to me that no one felt the others were being favored, so I kept track of who had gotten the best copy the week before and rotated the clean copy past all of them.

At one point I started sending roses to the girls on Valentine's Day. They went over big—it was a good investment. I started with Joann. None of them had steady boyfriends in those days, so I just got into the habit. It went on for years, until I decided it was the job of their husbands.

Chapter Four

Being Irish and being Catholic go hand in hand in our area, and people in our predominantly Catholic town tell First Communion stories the way others talk about births or marriages. First Communion is an important ritual in the Catholic Church. It's the second of the seven Sacraments and we took it seriously. In those days, when I received First Communion, everyone still fasted from midnight until Mass in the morning and communion time—so there was a lot of pressure not to eat or drink anything. My mom fainted because she had been fasting from midnight the night before. In some ways the Catholic Church is more lax now than when we were kids; in other ways, it's just the same, with lots of rules and regulations to keep you in line.

Everyone in the family, boys and girls, got a coconut-covered cake on their First Communion, always in the shape of a lamb: the symbol of innocence, purity, and the baby Jesus. It covered all the bases. Annie Donahue, our neighbor, made all of ours. The cake wasn't really made to be eaten, more of a centerpiece. Each of us also received a scapular on a ribbon to wear around the neck. The scapular held a picture of Jesus with long hair and a dark robe on one side and Mary with a halo of stars and wearing a sky-blue robe on the other. The pictures were covered with clear plastic and the whole piece was stitched together around the edges. The best gift of all was a special glow-in-the-dark rosary, nestled in a white box in soft cotton. I wore the big oval beads around my neck during the day, and at night they emitted an eerie green aura when I looked over the blanket edge and saw the rosary hanging on the headboard of the bed.

I was the fifth girl in the family to wear the First Communion dress. It was close to being a family heirloom. Pat, Mary Jo, and Kathy, Mom's sisters, had all come before my own sister Joann. The dress was embroidered organza with a couple of layers of full skirt, round collar, and puff sleeves. The veil was made out of my mother's wedding crown.

We had to study for weeks to be ready, attending special classes to prepare us not to embarrass our parents in case we were asked questions by the presiding parish priest. Catholic catechism is a rote study practice; memorization is everything. There isn't a Catholic in the United States who can't recite the prayers they learned as a child in catechism class, and I'm no exception.

After the First Communion Mass, we always invited relatives over for a meal—maybe brunch or lunch to celebrate, the crowd spilling out into the yard to sit with plates and cups balanced on their laps while the kids ran around and chased each other. For my First Communion, the reception was back at the house. Father Ginter, who had officiated at the rite, arrived not long after we did to continue the day's celebration. He was a white-haired priest who sometimes drove by in a VW bug and threw jawbreakers to kids in their yards. We scrambled through the grass to get them. We were close to the priests at the church. They often came to the house for dinner and were almost a part of the family. We made a point of inviting them; they lived alone and enjoyed a home-cooked meal.

Church was a special occasion—a special occasion every single week. Saturday evenings we all took baths, three or four kids to one tub of water, getting ready for Saturday evening Mass or Mass on Sunday morning. Everyone's hair was washed using a pitcher of water, and then rinsed with vinegar. It had to shine. The girls were in charge of getting all the shoes ready for church— black patent leather for us and black or brown leather for the boys. We sat on the stairs to the basement, facing backwards, so our legs could hang down between the steps and the step above us became a small table for our shoeshine workshop. We used paste wax for the boys' shoes. There was a technique we followed every single Saturday—put it on, let it dry, shine it. Shine, shine, shine. We used Vaseline for the girls' shoes. While we worked, others in the house would run up and down the steps—retrieving canned goods from the basement and fixing dinner in the kitchen above.

You had to dress up for church, and shiny shoes were only part of the outfit. The girls wore gloves and small hats. If you left your hat on the living room sofa on the way out the door, you wore a folded hanky on your head. Mom always managed to pull one out of her purse when she saw you looking under the seat in the car for the forgotten head covering.

Some people grow up Catholic and attend catechism classes on Sunday, but public school during the week. Not our family. I went to a Catholic grade school at a neighboring parish with twenty-one kids in my class. We knelt next to our desks at least once a week, and daily during Lent and Advent to say the rosary. The requisite posture was straight back with hands held at the chest moving the rosary beads through the fingers, one at a time, reciting out loud in unison: "Hail Mary, full of grace, the Lord is with you . . ." A full rosary includes fifty-three Hail Marys and six Our Fathers, plenty of time to slump to the side or sneak a moment's respite on the heels. Sister Inez of the Mercy Sisters, dressed in navy blue and white, was my teacher and wise to these tricks. She walked up and down the aisles between the desks and poked you in the back if you were slumping or not maintaining proper decorum during rosary.

From grade school, I went on to study at a Catholic junior high. We wore uniforms I could recognize as those of a Catholic schoolgirl anywhere in the world—a green plaid skirt, a white blouse, and a solid sweater. Each Catholic school had different colors, and we went to the local JCPenney's to buy our uniforms a few weeks before school started. They had racks of them, all new and crisp and arranged from largest to smallest. It didn't take long to choose the set, go home for Mom to sew our name tags in the collars and waistbands, and be ready for the new school year to begin.

My sister Patty was the kind of student who could horse around in class and everyone loved her. Even Sister Mary with the conservative dress and brown-laced shoes loved her. Me? I made Sister Mary cry. She swore she would quit being a teacher because of me. The real problem was that I could learn on my own, so I spent the time in class goofing around. I just wouldn't listen to Sister or honor her role as my teacher, someone I should be learning from. She wasn't creative enough to hold my attention. I expected a lot from myself and from those around me. I challenged authority quite a bit. If I lost respect for someone, I had a hard time faking it. I still do. One day I was feeling particularly feisty, and I made the class laugh by moving Sister's overhead projector so that the material was presented on the wall instead of the screen. We were unable to read it, but she had a habit of never looking up while she was teaching, so she wasn't aware that it had been moved until the end of class.

Frustration must have been building up in her for a while, because when she realized what I had done, she exploded. She cried, renounced her desire to continue as a teacher, and sent me to the principal's office.

I went into the girls' bathroom and sobbed. I couldn't stop. I just hid in one of the stalls and wouldn't come out. I was embarrassed that my behavior had been brought to the attention of the principal and other faculty. The story was inconsistent with my reputation, and I didn't like the other teachers hearing about it.

Later in the afternoon, I calmed down and managed to go back to class. When school was over that day, the gym teacher caught a glimpse of me in the hall and said, "I heard you made Sister Mary cry today." I knew it was a tease, but I started crying again, searching for the right moment to run away and hide. My sister Patty jumped right in and defended me.

"You don't even know the whole story," she told the gym teacher. "You stay out of this!"

Dad knew about me and what happened with Sister Mary, but I don't think he ever told Mom. He might have stood up for my bravado, but Mom would have been furious, if not heartbroken, to hear another story about her daughter with the mouthy attitude.

One day just before my first year in high school, a neighbor drove into the driveway and got out in a hurry. It was obviously important news; Mom and Dad were very serious. Aquin, the Catholic high school, was closing and becoming a public high school. My parents didn't even consider having us go to the "new" school. Instead, we were going to drive thirty minutes to Beckman, the Catholic high school in Dyersville, Iowa.

I didn't want to go to Beckman; only five of my classmates from Aquin were going and none of my close friends. Some of the neighbors said my parents "thought they were too good" to send their kids to the new public high school. That wasn't it. Mom and Dad were just insistent that we all get a Catholic education. We overheard many heated conversations over the uproar the whole issue caused in town, but there was never a question in our house about where we would be going to school. It was not an option for us to attend the new public school just because it was nearby. Mom and Dad lost friends over it.

Our family belonged to Sacred Heart Church in Fillmore. It stood out in the middle of nowhere, a rural church after all, less than a five-minute drive on the back roads from our house. It is a simple redbrick building with stained glass windows and a triangular spire topped by a white cross. Over the front doors were three white triangular cornices. There is a brass plaque on the front of the building with our family name. Will and Marie Curoe, my grandparents, had donated the money for restoration decades before. The cemetery to the side and behind the church was filled with the names of our neighbors and our relatives. Mom and Dad have four plots: two for them and two spares.

Chapter Five

My lack of awareness of Carol being a lesbian was probably rooted in my own background. I was born in 1925, the child of Irish Catholic parents, on a farm in a very conservative area of eastern Iowa. To understand our small community, one must know something of the history of Iowa itself.

The first white men who saw Iowa were the French Jesuit Father Marquette and Louis Joliet. In June 1673, they came down the mouth of the Wisconsin River, discovered the Mississippi, and faced the bluffs of the Iowa shore. Later, Catholic missionaries arrived from Quebec and worked alongside the Iowan Indians. They propagated the Catholic faith among pioneers and helped the faithful stay connected to their Catholic roots. The first Mass celebrated in the area that became Iowa was in 1833 in a private home in Dubuque, only sixteen miles from our home now. The first Catholic church in the state was built in Dubuque by the Dominican missionary Samuel Mazzuchelli in 1836.

Iowa became United States territory as part of the Louisiana Purchase in 1803, and in 1833, after a treaty with the Indians, was opened to settlement. The earliest

Catholic settlers were French, German, and Irish. Many arrived directly from their native countries, eager to settle the area that lay between the Mississippi and the Missouri Rivers, the region that fast became known as the Great Central Plains. Even today, the heritage of our Iowa neighbors is 42 percent German and 37 percent Irish.

The legacy of those first settlers flows in our veins today, and we are Catholics to the core. Aunts on both sides of the family are nuns, and there's a priest in there somewhere. I have two sisters who also became nuns. I was an altar boy and did exactly what Sister Celeste, the principal of the school, told me to do.

The first talk of homosexuality I recall hearing was when I was drafted into the armed services and it was considered grounds for deferment. In all my years of Catholic education, I have no memory of knowing anyone that was gay. Even the subject of homosexuality was off limits in our house, though my parents were more liberal than many neighbors at that time. My parents were in the forefront of equal rights for African Americans and Native Americans despite the fact that we lived in a 100 percent white community. They made it clear they thought discrimination against any group was wrong, and we knew you should never disparage or make fun of another ethnic group or race. When it came to homosexuality, my parents agreed with the Catholic Church that it was a grievous sin, and they wouldn't tolerate any discussion about the topic. I believe it was because they didn't believe in putting people down, mocking or dehumanizing them. Hired men would tell snickering jokes and be told, "We don't talk like that in this house." My parents didn't want their children hearing it, not because it was about a group they felt repelled by, but because it was against their value of decency to make other human beings a target of disdain and hate.

In school I don't remember any children who could be retrospectively identified as "gay," but there was always the negative stereotype around—certain male inflections and gestures that spelled out "homosexual." I don't know where that stereotyping comes from, whether kids pick it up from their parents or an odd comment on the street, but I didn't need anyone to tell me what it meant. I intuitively knew it was not the thing to do if you didn't want to stand out and become the focus of someone's ridicule. Looking back, I'm sure I knew at least a few homosexuals, but at the time I didn't recognize it or identify it. I knew several adults who never married, so it leaves the door open for wondering. Of course, it wasn't so unusual during those years for men and women not to marry. Irish men married young or didn't marry at all. It was the Depression, and a lot of people bonded with their brothers and sisters. They shared houses with extended families, shared cars and even jobs during desperate times when unemployment ran rampant. This was easier and more economical.

Coming out as homosexual was unusual for anyone in those years. Even if people just *thought* a person was "out," it created huge problems for them. If my parents were alive today, I can't imagine their reaction if they knew they had a lesbian granddaughter.

I carried my Catholic values and upbringing into my own family once I got married. We were active in the community, helping out at church and raising money for different projects along the way. This included trying to keep the local Catholic high school going. The high school was in a bad financial situation and the board had to raise $75,000 or it would close. That amount of money doesn't sound like much now, but thirty years ago it was a great deal and this isn't the big city. It's a farming community where the annual income for many families often hovers just above the federal poverty line. Many of the parents went out to help raise the funds, but we just couldn't get the job done. We did all of the usual fund-raising you associate with a church. We held bake sales and car washes, but that kind of fund-raising doesn't go very far in bringing in large sums of money. Joyce and I wanted that school to stay open. We pledged $1,000. It closed in 1976.

Today, we still have two good elementary school systems in our area—one parochial and one public. Even though our children have been long gone from the local schools, I have been heavily involved in the effort to get the fund-raising off the ground for a new parochial school facility. We've raised $3.8 million so far—we're almost there.

PART III

Detour

Chapter Six

I wasn't even out of school at Marquette before I realized that engineering wasn't for me, but I still graduated from the program. I headed into a field I thought would be more fitting to my talents and personality—business management. I planned to take my engineering degree and parlay it into a career that spoke more to my heart than designing buildings, bridges, and highways. I moved to Phoenix, Arizona, and enrolled in a well-known international business school—a school that had students from all over the world fine-tuning their résumés with high-level business management skills.

While I finished graduate school, I got a part-time job at a large national engineering and architectural design firm. The work reassured me in a strange way. It wasn't what I wanted to be doing for a career and reinforced my decision to go into business. What could I possibly have been thinking when I selected civil engineering as a major?

Yet, the job was great work while I was in graduate school, and I was getting experience that would look good on my résumé. I worked twenty hours per week and went to school full-time. There were a lot of new engineering graduates in the office, everyone buzzing about weekend plans and where they were going to hang out after work. As a part-timer, I wasn't really included in all the fun and social activities.

One slow Monday morning I sat in my office cube working diligently on locating existing utilities for a major interchange that was to be built in downtown Phoenix. I'd had another quiet weekend talking to friends and family in Iowa on the phone, studying, and spending time with some classmates. That morning I felt every bit the outsider that I was. I wasn't even on the fringe of the social life at the office—I was completely beyond it. One of the full-time engineers, Susan, was just the opposite. Her desk was in a high-traffic area, and I noticed that everyone who passed her desk stopped to say hello and talk about the weekend they'd just had or the one coming up. No one stayed very long, but with all of the visits combined, I couldn't imagine she was getting any work accomplished.

One particularly busy Monday morning, I made a copy of the company's one-page phone list and wrote a message across the top of the page: "Please check off your name after speaking with Susan." I attached a string to a pencil and taped it to the phone list. Then I waited patiently for a break in the action before walking over to Susan's office cube. I casually pinned the phone list to her wall where it was clearly visible to everyone who walked past. We both laughed, friendly, but polite. After all, we didn't really know each other very well.

I went back to my cube alone and congratulated myself for being very funny. I had a good laugh at my witty
way of getting in on the fun at work, even though I didn't
share it with anyone. I didn't define what I had just done
as flirting. Why would anyone flirt with a person of the
same sex?

A few months later, as graduation was rapidly approaching, my classmates were focused on finding high-powered,
high-paying jobs befitting someone with an MBA from a
well-known international institution. Not me, though.
The list on the wall had done the trick. I'd broken through
and had finally worked myself into the in crowd at work.
I was so busy partying that just graduating with my MBA
became enough of a challenge. Getting a job would have
to wait.

The only thing I was doing that could be considered
job-search-related was talking to the human resources
director at the engineering firm where I worked during
graduate school. She was feeding me information about
a full-time position in San Jose, California. Yes, it was an
engineering position, and yes, I went to graduate school
to avoid becoming one of those geeky engineers with
pocket protectors. But California was still a draw. When
you grow up in the Midwest, California can sound almost exotic. I was sure that once I was out there, I could
move out of engineering and into employment more related to business. I followed up on the job lead, sending
my résumé and references. I got deep enough into the

process to visit the San Jose office and begin negotiating salary and relocation reimbursement. But I still had some questions as to whether it was the right move.

By now, Susan and I had become best friends. We were known throughout the office for our superior social planning abilities, and we seemed always to be in the middle of some prank, organizing company outings or replaying the details of a recent party. I dialed her extension to see if she would take a break with me. I wanted to talk about this potential move with someone who knew me well. I needed to run it by a friend who could help me be clear about what I was contemplating doing and why. She met me at my desk, and we walked across the street to our favorite frozen yogurt shop and bought our regulars.

I wasn't too far into the conversation when Susan stopped me and told me she had also applied for the same position in California. I was dumbfounded. What she was saying didn't make any sense. She knew I was applying for the job and she chose to compete with me. She avoided my eyes. She was obviously uncomfortable, but why would she do such a thing? In truth, I hadn't told her not to. It just never occurred to me that a friend would even consider going after the same job. She suggested there was a chance both of us would get an offer. This also made no sense. From the information I had gotten from the company and the HR director, I could only conclude Susan had made that up to rationalize her strange, disloyal behavior.

In the end, I didn't take the job and neither did Susan.

I decided I didn't want to leave the social network I had in Phoenix and move alone to San Jose. I changed my status at the engineering firm from part-time to full-time after getting my MBA and tried to convince myself I deserved to enjoy some time without school or the pressures of a full-out job search. I wasn't successful. I beat myself up emotionally for taking a job I could have had without spending time and money on graduate school. I was still so deep in denial about the real motivations working in the background of my life, it never occurred to me I might have stayed in that job so I could continue my friendship with Susan. Who would allow a close personal friendship to influence important career decisions?

Lake Powell stretches hundreds of miles from Lees Ferry, Arizona, to the orange, yellow, and tan lands of Utah. We rounded up camping gear, planned food for four days, and caravanned in three cars with twelve people from Phoenix for a weekend of partying, waterskiing, hiking, and hanging out on the water. Lake Powell is a man-made wonder filled with sky-blue, crystal-clear water as deep as its walls are high—a likely partner for the neighboring Grand Canyon, carved from orange, red, and purple stone. We found a great campsite on a secluded spot along the shore, unloaded the cars, and dug in.

We got into our swimming suits, slapped on the sunscreen, rented a boat, and water-skied. I was the only one in the group who knew how to ski or drive a motorboat, but everyone was game to try it. The contrast of sliding over the water with the magnificent landforms as a backdrop made for a surreal experience. My days as a water-ski instructor at Lake Kamaji, a girl's camp outside of Bemidji, Minnesota, just after college served me well. I had almost everyone up on skis at least for a short distance. After a couple of days of pulling beginner skiers, however, I was ready to ski myself, and our friend Joe was willing to drive the boat for me.

I gave him some simple instructions: "When I say, 'Hit it!' just push the throttle all the way forward and don't let up until I'm on top of the water and I give you a thumbs-down signal. If I give you a thumbs-up signal, that means go a little faster."

Other than those basic directions, I was sure I could handle whatever driving Joe delivered. We took off, me slowly rising out of the water on one ski and holding the towrope with one hand. I zipped over the water, sending out a rooster tail spray to the right and the left, laughing as my friends waved back at me from the boat. I could see Susan cheering me on. I enjoyed the attention I was getting from a boat full of beginning skiers and decided they would appreciate a show of my real skiing skills. I zoomed back and forth over the boat's wake, getting some air between me and Lake Powell, leaning to the side as my arms stretched out in front of me.

I gave Joe the thumbs-up to go faster. I was a star and then I was a wipeout.

The impact with the water knocked me unconscious.

I floated, faceup. I heard later that Joe jerked back the throttle and almost sent the rest of the passengers flying out of the boat. He circled around to where I was bobbing in the water. As they came alongside, Susan jumped out of the boat, without a life jacket. Later she explained how dismayed she was that no one else was taking action to do anything. I came to and opened my eyes just as she landed next to me.

"What are you doing?" I lectured as I turned over to tread water. "You never jump in to help someone without a jacket, even if you can swim!" All those years of swim lessons made my response almost automatic.

My reaction took Susan by surprise. She paddled back to the boat and climbed up the ladder like a chastised child with hurt feelings. The passengers handed down a towel and helped her in. She didn't speak and neither did anyone else. They were all stunned by my accident, but probably as much so by my insensitive, uncharacteristic outburst.

My denial over my relationship with Susan had kicked in again. I still didn't understand why she had applied for the same job I did in San Jose, and I didn't probe my own psyche to understand why a friend who doesn't swim well risked her own life to jump into thirty feet of water to save me.

Not long after our trip to Lake Powell, I realized what was going on with Susan's unusual behavior. She was in love, and while it still took me a while to figure it out, I was too. Although I had dated off and on through high school and college, I had never come close to being in love before. I had never experienced the emotional high of adoring someone, being fascinated by everything they did and said, and having that person echo the feelings back to me. It was an exuberant, wild ride.

Over the next weeks and months we spent all of our time together. I was very honest with Susan and made sure that she knew I wasn't a lesbian, though I was definitely enjoying the experience of being in love. In my heart, I felt sorry for her. We talked about how it was an unfortunate event that two friends just happened to get "too close." I suspected that maybe she was, in fact, a lesbian even if she didn't acknowledge it yet.

I was honest with Susan the whole time. I never pretended to feel any way I didn't or to have more hope for our relationship past this brief time of enjoying each other. Being completely honest with her required that we talk about how and when our relationship would end. The end was inevitable, of course, since I was not a lesbian and eventually others would start to suspect our relationship. My parents would be devastated. I was not the kind of girl to do something this offensive. Most of my life so far had involved trying to make my parents proud by pursuing a series of activities that spelled out conventional success from many different directions: high school salutatorian, volleyball and basketball captain, student council, and female engineer. I might have been a feisty kid and a bit outspoken to the nuns, but embarrassing my parents and family by being a lesbian was not part of that plan.

We talked a lot about why we needed to put the brakes on our relationship. We each spent anxious days and sleepless nights mulling over the euphoria of being in love, coupled with the horror of anyone finding out. We bonded even more during teary conversations. I reprimanded myself constantly by thinking, This has got to stop. I have to be more self-disciplined. We've made a choice to have fun together. We don't need to be in love with each other, we choose to do it. We can also choose to stop.

Multiple attempts at ending the relationship met with no success. We separated for hours at best, going off with a new resolve and ending up back together holding hands, in each other's arms by the end of the day.

I took the analytical high road. I needed to get away for a while. I would distance myself from the situation, make a rational decision, and come up with the appropriate action plan. I talked to a friend who had a sister-in-law living in San Diego and asked for time off from work. All I needed was some time on the beach to sort things out.

I cried most of the time I was in sunny, glorious San Diego. The woman I was staying with wasn't around much, so she didn't have the opportunity to see a near stranger fall apart. I watched straight couples holding hands on the beach and resented them for their ability to do that publicly. I saw women hanging out together, eating dinner, running on the sand and tried to guess if they had lesbian relationships like the one I was leaving, the one that didn't fit for me, the one that was a farce because I wasn't a lesbian, I was merely a young woman who had fallen in love.

Susan and I talked on the phone every night and often several times during the day. We talked about small things happening at work, the weather, and how we were going to stay away from each other.

I made a plan. The first thing I had to do was move out of the apartment we shared. I called a friend in Phoenix who was planning an extended vacation and asked to rent his apartment. Next I would get a different job to create even more distance between Susan and me. I called my previous employer who had an office in town to see if they had openings. They did. I arranged to start working there shortly after I got back from San Diego.

Everything was set. My heart and mind were settled. Now I could drive back to Phoenix.

The night I arrived, I was surprised at how Susan looked. The week I had spent in San Diego seemed even harder on her than it was on me. She had lost ten pounds, close to 10 percent of her total weight. I on the other hand, had gained ten pounds. Susan hadn't slept much either, and she looked pretty rough; pale skin, dark circles under her eyes. But it had to be done. We reviewed the plan one more time and decided tomorrow would be soon enough to put it into action.

I took the new job, but we couldn't end the relationship. Moonlight came into our bedroom and filled the whole room. It was romantic and soothing. Every night we ended up together. I never moved into my friend's apartment. The new job didn't provide much distance, either, since it was directly across the parking lot from the old one, where Susan still worked.

Susan's thirtieth birthday was approaching. She wanted to go away for a nice quiet weekend—just the two of us. Fortunately, or unfortunately at this time, we had a lot of good friends. They wanted to put together something big for her milestone birthday. Planning a quiet romantic getaway became almost impossible; keeping the complex stories straight associated with our planning became a supreme challenge.

Eventually, a group of twelve friends helped me arrange a surprise weekend up north for Susan. The plan was for them to leave earlier than us on a Friday night, take all the food, get checked in, and wait quietly for us to show up. They wanted to know what story I would use to get Susan up north with enough clothes for a weekend and still have it be a surprise. When I told them she thought it was just going to be the two of us, I got quizzical looks. Why would Susan, the social planner, want to do that? Why wasn't she inviting her best friends for a weekend up north? I made up a weak excuse about her needing some space. It didn't ring true, even to me.

In the face of their confusion, I tried to convince her to invite our friends or let me do so. I didn't want them to get suspicious about our relationship. But Susan was afraid that if we invited anyone, they might actually say yes. I tried to convince her we were safe to invite them because they already had plans and would say no. She was adamant about keeping it a quiet weekend for just the two of us.

We arrived about 11:00 P.M. It was one of those dark nights in the woods, when you see familiar constellations above the treetops and the air is light and crisp. We opened the cabin door, lugging our bags, and switched on the light.

"Surprise!" Twelve friends jumped out from behind the furniture and thrust through the bedroom doors.

Susan's expression was captured on film: clear horror.

Later she told me she was sure everyone had "found out" about us. She thought our friends were announcing that they knew we were a couple. She recovered quickly when she realized the surprise was for her birthday and not her sexual orientation. She was the social princess after all and kicked into the party mode. The weekend passed quickly. We golfed, cooked dinners together, and laughed. And then we loaded up the cars and headed back to the desert. We had not only survived another possible outing of our relationship, but had grown stronger in the face of it.

Our relationship continued, but I still knew it would end. I just didn't know when. It was impossible for me to envision anything else. I knew I would get married to a man and have kids. There was no thought of "coming out." I reserved that for real lesbians. We continued to hide our relationship, and Susan even went on a date or two to maintain our cover. I still wasn't the dating kind.

One weekend we rented a cabin in beautiful Sedona, Arizona, north of Phoenix. After checking in and getting settled, we hiked along the creek. We sat on a big red sandstone rock overlooking the creek, watching the sun through the trees. We talked about our relationship, commiserating with each other. Susan was particularly anxious. We cried. We felt sorry for ourselves and talked about the fact that we could have no life together. What were we going to do?

I repeated the truth I had been stating all along. This was the first time I had really been in love, and it was unfortunate it had to be with a woman.

"There are lots of choices out there in the world for relationships," I said. "For me, this isn't one of them."

"It isn't a choice for me," said Susan.

"What do you mean, it isn't a choice for you? That doesn't make any sense. Of *course* it's your choice."

"I've suspected I was a lesbian since I was in junior high school." Susan leaned over the edge of the boulder, looking at the water, not at me. My head spun, grappling for a response that would save the day, save me. I felt I could make her take it back, say it the right way. "I always thought I just needed to meet the right guy," she continued.

I was sick to my stomach.

I processed what she said silently for a few moments.

I get what I want by being methodical, logical. Very, very clear about how I feel. "This changes everything that's been going on between us. You've tricked me."

She had baited me back when we first met at the engineering firm. She had trapped me in this relationship, by pretending (or at least agreeing with me) that it was a lark, just two friends who got too close. My anger and fear rushed in and filled the moment. We were eighteen months into the relationship, and what Susan had just said was the ultimate betrayal. While I suspected she was a lesbian, somehow knowing she had thought about it all this time made it seem more premeditated and conniving.

"I love you, but you need to know this isn't going anywhere," I said. My voice was steely cold. I'm not the type to yell. "I am not a lesbian," I repeated. I felt sorry for her. She's stuck in this mess because she's a lesbian, I thought. But I'm not.

Susan told me later she had been scared for weeks that the whole thing was going to blow up in her face. She said it felt safer to keep her mouth shut about feelings she had had since seventh grade. She was right. My reaction was exactly what she had feared. Self-righteous. Calculating. An emotional run for the hills. I finally had my way out of this relationship.

We finished the weekend in Sedona with anxiety and confusion.

We loved each other.

It was over.

Upon our return from Sedona, I went to a social worker for counseling. I needed to figure out how to get out of this relationship for good. I clearly wasn't doing it on my own. I was able to be very clear with the social worker. "Help me get out of this."

The social worker took me into territory I thought was unrelated. She got me talking about alcoholism and denial. I thought we were digressing from the problem at hand—that I had been trapped by Susan in this relationship and needed some language for ending it and going on with my life—my life as a heterosexual woman. The social worker was quicker than me. She picked up early on that I was well versed in alcoholism. From an early age, Mom made sure we understood the signs and risks of alcoholism. We understood the hold alcohol could have on individuals and the power of denial in these situations.

The social worker didn't waste any time. She used alcohol and denial as an analogy to open my eyes to the possibility that perhaps I was in denial about my own sexuality.

"Do you think there is a chance you are gay, and that perhaps you have been all your life?" she asked.

I was dumbfounded, but only for a few minutes. The door opened and I walked right through. Memories of earlier crushes on girls came flooding back to me. I had never thought of them as crushes, because crushes were only feelings you had for someone of the opposite sex. I didn't think I could be a lesbian because lesbians wore leather and rode motorcycles. They could hurt me! In all the years of high school and college, one of my biggest fears was that people would think I was gay when I really wasn't.

I got home about 7:00 P.M., and the stories spilled out. Susan and I talked for hours. We found common ground we had never had until that night.

Over the next weeks, I brought my usual academic and detail-oriented personality to the mix. If I was going to be one of "them," I was going to learn about them. I found a gay and lesbian bookstore and we invested in a small library. I read everything I could get my hands on and met myself anew on every page. The pieces of my life fit together for the first time. I still didn't like it, but at least now I was dealing with the whole picture. I began to accept my responsibility for being in this relationship instead of blaming and holding Susan accountable for it.

Susan and I exchanged rings in San Diego on July 1, 1989, two years after we met in Phoenix. It was a marriage in our minds, anyway. A jeweler we met at an art fair made the rings. We didn't dare have both rings made the same, although we both liked a malachite ring the best. I chose a blue lapis. We were two women getting married. We wore the rings on our right hands, afraid to wear them on the left and incite comment from friends or family.

Our wedding night, we stayed at Dana Point Resort, an upscale hotel in Dana Point, California. Susan wore a red silk dress with long sleeves, fitted with a pleated skirt. I wore a white suit with a long pleated skirt and a royal blue silk blouse. We went out on the patio. Susan brought out wedding wine glasses and two wedding cake figures. They had been sets with both a man and a woman. She had cut them apart and put the two women together.

We set the camera self-timer.

We exchanged vows we had written ourselves.

Afterward, we went out for dinner and drank too much. We were sorry for ourselves, even in the midst of our happiness. We were alone, and we couldn't really get married. The alcohol and the tension of the decision made us melancholy and sad.

We bought a house together in Phoenix. Dad thought we should take title as tenants in common, purchase it as individuals, and share the costs. Susan and I wanted to be joint tenants. If either of us died, the title would pass to the other. Dad explained his rationale for tenants in common clearly, but we went ahead with our own plan. This was one of the first times I remember going against Dad's advice. I understood why he was perplexed by our decision, but I knew he didn't have the whole picture either.

Chapter Seven

We knew Susan quite well by the time we received Carol's letter. She and Carol had lived together for almost five years, first sharing an apartment and then purchasing a home together in Phoenix. We had even visited Susan's parents in Crystal Lake, Illinois. But still, to say we were shocked by the news that they were lesbians would be an understatement.

After a week or two, I called Susan's parents and talked to her father, Jim. We knew Susan had sent her parents a letter the same day Carol wrote to us. We had a long conversation in which I told Jim that neither Joyce nor I blamed Susan for Carol's coming out. In hindsight, I can admit I did somewhat blame Susan, and that is why I raised the issue with her father. He was no happier with the news than I was. They hadn't known Susan was a lesbian and took the news very hard. I think this helped Joyce and me rise to the occasion—we decided to set a tone for talking to Susan and Carol and a tone of working through it, as hard as it was. We knew it was going to be important for others to see how we reacted. If we were angry and turned against Carol, we could expect others who were close to us, and even those we barely knew, to follow suit. After all, we were the parents. If we didn't support our daughter, why should anyone else?

Every year, one of the kids invites us to have Christmas at their home. They take turns. We had already accepted Carol's invitation to have Christmas with her in Phoenix that year. With the news of her coming out, we considered not going. We weren't sure if we were ready. The easy way seemed to be to come up with an excuse. In the end, we decided to go because we were afraid that if we didn't, they would take it as rejection. On previous visits, they each appeared to have their own bedroom in their two-bedroom house. When we arrived, Susan would move into Carol's room and give us her bedroom. We had never thought anything about it except that it was a thoughtful thing to do. It would obviously be different this time.

We went to Mass on Christmas Eve, and I went for a run on Christmas morning. When I came back, Carol, Susan, and Joyce were sitting outside on their patio, laughing. There had been a grease fire in the oven and the turkey was ruined. Susan's sense of humor eased the tension, and she got the blame for what seemed like a disaster at the time. What could have been a very uncomfortable weekend, even a catastrophe, was actually quite pleasant. The visit was somewhat stilted, but overall it went a long way toward Susan becoming part of the Curoe family.

I reminded myself frequently that Susan and Carol were the same people they were before we received the letter. At night, Joyce and I talked about the day; we replayed conversations and worried about how we handled them. Would we ever be comfortable with this situation? I now understand that many people have done far worse than we did in such situations, some even going so far as to cut their gay children out of their lives, for years, or even forever.

One such conversation happened while playing cards, Joyce miscounted trump. Susan had one trump left that Joyce didn't anticipate. "You can't have trump left!" Joyce said.

"Is the Pope Catholic?" shot back Susan. This line could usually be counted on to get a laugh, but not this time.

Joyce looked Susan directly in the eyes and said, "I hope so. I've based my entire life on it." The table froze. It was Susan's first experience with our strong Catholic faith, and it put an abrupt end to the lighthearted card game.

On the last day of our five-day visit, Carol and Joyce stood at the kitchen counter talking about how the visit went. We had thought it would be tense, how could it not be? We were all staying in a house, having Christmas, with our lesbian daughter and her girlfriend. But the truth was, the event was not so much different than any other time we had spent with Susan and Carol. We laughed. We talked. We went on walks. We fixed dinner together.

In a parting conversation, Joyce was serious as she told Carol, "I have always loved Susan and thought of her as part of our family. It's just that I didn't picture her as a son-in-law."

Chapter Eight

We wrote the letters in September. September 13, 1990, to be exact.

We had chosen this time to write letters to both sets of parents precisely because of Christmas. We were through being apart on holidays and pretending it didn't matter. Our siblings often talked at family get-togethers about their boyfriends or girlfriends, and of course their spouses would be there. Often, the boyfriends or girlfriends would join us for a special meal or even for several days. Everyone joined in the banter and the questions to cheer on the burgeoning relationships. I found myself happy for my siblings and my own heart aching for the life I was living that I couldn't share without creating havoc in my life. The thought of one more holiday being with loved family and carving out the time for an intimate phone conversation with Susan late in the night was depressing. We literally got tired of it.

Susan and I each wrote our own letter, sitting at the dining room table, hour after hour, draft after draft. We had to make multiple copies, one for every member of our immediate families. Mine would go to three brothers and two sisters, plus my parents. Susan's would be sent to her two brothers and her parents. Susan was more confident in her letter to her family. She had had more than a decade to think about it, having suspected since junior high that she was a lesbian. After a couple of serious relationships with men, she was much more resigned to the fact that she would eventually need to accept who she was. In a way, she had been preparing herself for the family's reaction for years. I had only defined myself as such a few years before.

My letter was much longer than Susan's and focused on my hopes and expectations for how my family might come to accept Susan and me as a lesbian couple. It was time to stop the facade that we were only best friends with no intimate, romantic connection. In some respects, it was a repeat of a letter I had written to Susan months before. I was on a business trip and penned a long, rambling scenario that lived in my fantasy. We would live together, have a family, and be accepted by our own families. In that letter, I was letting my best dreams go out into the universe, willing them to be true. Now I was writing a letter to take one more step in the process, and I was scared.

When the letters were sealed, stamped, and surrendered to the post office bin, the anticipated sense of relief turned to fear. We became players in an intense waiting game. Over the next days, we went to our jobs filled with tension. We knew when the mail arrived at our parents' homes and when the letters might be in their mailboxes. I knew when Dad would finish with the chores and possibly leave a phone call. Instead, his initial response was a fax sent to my office. It was the most impersonal communication I have ever received from either of my parents. Instead of relief, it simply confirmed what a huge deal this was.

Each night we came back to the house and weren't home two minutes before we checked the mail and looked at the answering machine to see the blinking light that signified a call. For days the red blinking light wasn't a message from my parents. It was our friends calling to see if we'd heard from my parents. Finally, one of these messages was from Mom. She started out with a strong voice, but then trailed off in tears. "We'll call when we can."

There was no going back. You don't write your parents a letter one week saying you are lesbian and then decide to take it back the next.

Our good friends had as much anxiety over the situation as we did. Those who were gay were disconnected from their own families, so we had no lead to follow in how to approach our siblings and parents. The stories we heard in those weeks laid the groundwork for what we have come to see as a theme in the gay community in terms of family support: "If you don't have a good family before coming out, you're not going to have a good one afterwards."

My parents finally called about a week after they received the letter, ten days after we sent it. Four of our friends were at our house for a dinner party. They were the first lesbians Susan and I had met when we came out to ourselves. The room grew very quiet and everyone strained to pick up on what was happening in the conversation, what my parents were saying on the other end. We were ahead of our friends, as most still hadn't told their parents they were lesbians. My parents' response was going to be a symbol of hope or fear, depending on how negatively they were affected and whether they found it in their hearts to support us. There was not even a chance that my parents might say, "What wonderful news! You're a lesbian. How thrilled we are for you. Marriage? Possibly children on the way? Tell us more."

When I got back to the table, the whole group was primed, ready for the information. The conversation with my parents had been tense, but it was a beginning. They told me they loved me. They were having a very hard time. We could talk more at a later time. I didn't feel much like being social, and the party broke up shortly thereafter with some hugs and words of encouragement.

These times of being together through the coming-out weeks and months became seminal moments in our friendships with the women who waited with us and supported us. In the same way you bond with people when there is a death or a natural disaster, our friendships grew stronger from these deep, shared events.

We had come out to my sisters Patty and Joann before we even sent the letter, so they were prepared. By the time my parents called, I had already talked to every sibling. To say each of the experiences was positive would be a stretch, though my brothers and sisters were supportive—the attitude was, "We'll all get through this together."

Thoughts of Christmas, still months away, consumed us. Would my parents come to our house, or would they change their plans?

Chapter Nine

I received the letter from Carol and went back to rake hay, weighing what my next move would be, should be. I looked across the fields at one of the earliest indicators of the changing seasons—the red and purplish colors of the various weeds along the roadsides—and then took the folded letter out of my pocket and reread it. It couldn't be true. Carol was a promising person—we had plans for her. She was unusually bright and sensitive, well motivated. I tried to decide how I could respond, when in truth I wanted to give no response at all.

That night I wrote two letters. I was sure I couldn't talk to Carol without crying, so I decided to send the short letter by fax, from our accountant's office in town the next day. In the morning, I drove the twenty miles to town in a daze, still unable to believe what I had read. At the accountant's office, I greeted the receptionist and headed to the fax machine, which sat on a table in the waiting room for the use of clients. I slipped my letter into the holder, glad there was no one else present who might possibly glance over and see what I had written, guess that my family was now very different than it had been just a few hours before.

Carol Curoe,

Your letter was received yesterday and this note is to tell you I have written and mailed you a response this A.M.

Your brother and family were here over the weekend and went from here to Chicago. He played twenty-seven holes of golf Saturday; nine with me in the morning and eighteen with the family in the afternoon.

Always,
Bob

Looking back now, I see how impersonal it was. But, at the time it was the best I could do. I returned home just as Joyce was leaving a message for Carol on her answering machine.

"Carol, this is your mother. I just wanted you to know we received your letter yesterday . . ." She began to weep again.

"I can't talk right now." Her voice halted, started again, and then broke through the crying. "But we'll call when we can."

"Sorry . . . We love you . . ."

As I watched Joyce weeping, I knew I should also respond. I sent my second letter of the day.

Dear Carol,

Your letter of the 13th greeted me at noon today. If I were to tell you I was happy with the contents it would be an out and out lie.

I read the letter, reread the letter, and read it again this evening. Most of the afternoon as I raked hay at the Martinsens' farm, in the strips where we rode horses on Labor Day, I wondered how to respond to the letter, or if I should. I recalled my father teaching me to accept decisions and events in life which I could not control. Over the years it has been sound advice when we would have excessive rains, droughts, or sick livestock that went with farming.

I'm sure you and Susan gave much thought to how you would like to share your lives, and the fact that I may or may not be happy or understand your decision does not mean I can't live with it or continue to love you. Accepting and approving of the situation, however, is a real challenge. Another saying from my dad is that time heals all sorrows. I hope he is right.

I have lost much sleep over the years because of decisions I made that turned out to be mistakes, and how I react to this news could also be one I'll regret. What I am trying to say, and probably am not doing a very good job of it, is that how you and Susan conduct your lives, careers, religious life, etc., is not any of my business.

We will call—I'm not sure when. Feel free to call first. I'm not mad at anybody, and I won't shout or curse into the phone if you call. You and Susan will always be welcome at our house and considered part of the family as you requested.

As I read this over, see the mistakes, I ask myself if I should send it or dump it in the wastebasket. It *doesn't seem to say much, yet your letter called for an immediate response. Sort of like the days you were in college and I wrote every week.*

Love,
Dad

   P.S. Carol, I would not feel I have been honest and straightforward with you and Susan if I mailed this and did not tell you your letter was much, much, much more difficult for Joyce than for me. If you would have asked me over Labor Day, I would have begged you to keep your life a secret from Joyce.
   Please try not to think that I am coming on too strong or just trying to make you feel bad. As you well know, Joyce is very proud, and has always been extremely proud of the family, sometimes too much so in my mind. I am at a complete loss as to what to say or do for her.

Always,
Dad

   Joyce has read the entire letter except for the above P.S. In your words as you and I looked at the four walls of an elevator at Mercy Hospital when Joyce had her heart attack a few years ago, "Oh, shit."

For days I fought back tears. I could hardly risk seeing friends or neighbors, there was such a block in my throat. I was afraid someone would mention Carol's name and I would be unable to control my emotions.

Joyce and I had scores of questions and no answers. What would society do to Carol? Where in my family did this come from? Why did this happen? Where had Joyce and I failed? How can we face the neighbors? Carol had sixteen years of Catholic schooling. Did the schools fail her also? What brought this event into our lives?

I recalled the weekly letters I wrote to her while she was college, and it only made the hurt worse. It reminded me of the true friendship Carol and I had while she was growing up. I feared things would never be the same again. I knew we wouldn't be shouting or fighting, but I also suspected the closeness was gone and could never be reclaimed.

On the outside, each day was like the others that came before. I worked on the farm, tended the animals, and Joyce took care of the house. But inside, I was filled with confusion and dread. I kept hoping it was a mistake. I would surely wake up from the bad dream. I couldn't organize my thoughts enough to trust myself in a conversation with Carol. I was her father, so I would never be cruel, but I had to be honest when I talked to her. I didn't know what "honest" was in this situation.

After an excruciating ten days, I called Carol late in the evening. I was ready to hear her voice. When she answered the phone and started to talk, I cried into the phone. She and Susan had friends over for dinner, so it was a short and difficult conversation.

After that phone call, the weeks went by very slowly. I talked to different members of the family in the evening.

Some of them were having trouble also. We were in a daze and didn't know how much to let this unbalance our lives. After all, it was a relationship between two young people—it was possible they would go their separate ways and the furor and anxiety would have been for no reason. Looking back, we should have told everyone immediately to "bite the bullet" and get behind Carol.

Joyce cried whenever she was alone. She would emerge from her room or the yard with the now familiar red eyes and stricken face. Patty called while Joyce was in the basement. When Joyce came up the stairs, I asked her if she wanted to talk to Patty about what was happening. She shook her head and broke down sobbing. Patty's response was immediate: "I'm coming home." I talked her out of it—there was nothing she could do. Joann knew, too. They both knew before we did. Joann was living in a conservative community, and she was a teacher, afraid to go public with the information that her sister was a lesbian.

We knew the Catholic Church opposed homosexuality—that was our primary reference point. We started paying a lot more attention to what the Church's statements said about gays and lesbians. Our son Michael, who had a Jesuit education, was perhaps the most supportive family member in the beginning. Later, support would come from unexpected sources. My sisters are Catholic nuns. They found articles for us about lesbianism and passed them on. We welcomed this perspective, but still were afraid of the general public's response.

Every day brought up new fears and questions. All we thought about was the letter, as we struggled to understand how Carol could do this to us or to her own life. She had always been a high achiever and easily made us proud parents. We worried about her personal safety, potential harassment, employment, and even her soul. Our biggest fear was that the neighbors would learn about Carol being a lesbian. They might paint our fence with obscenities, just like in Dubuque a few years before when the community exploded with slurs against African Americans.

Joyce and I were in complete agreement about one thing: we could not tell anyone.

Five days after Carol's letter arrived, there was a family wedding. Joyce said she didn't know how she could possibly get through it. At that stage, however, we were stunned and stoic. The hand-wringing came later.

The thought of Carol being gay had not crossed my mind before the letter arrived. Joyce was ahead of me in tuning into the possibilities. One summer, Carol had invited Susan to join our family vacation, saying that Susan would be in the Midwest anyway. It seemed fine; we all enjoyed Susan's company. Joyce, suspecting in some part of her mind that Carol was attracted to women, confronted her as they lay on the crowded beach.

"Is there any 'lesbianish' activity going on between you and Susan?" she asked.

"No, of course not, Mom," was Carol's response. Joyce got the answer she wanted and was allowed to continue in her own denial. Looking back, there were a number of indications that, had I been open to seeing them, would have made Carol's announcement less of a shock. When Susan and Carol were buying a house I was surprised to learn they took ownership as joint tenants instead of as tenants in common. This seemed unusual to me at the time and from a business standpoint didn't seem wise, but Carol was determined.

"Appearance means a lot to me," Joyce said to me once the letter arrived. "Women looking like men—that sort of thing doesn't appeal to me, and I don't like public affection where gays are flaunting their choice for all to see."

At the same time, Joyce was concerned for Carol and Susan. She remarked that it was clear how much they loved each other, and she knew that if they broke up, it would be terribly hard for both of them.

After our initial shock, Joyce and I began the healing journey. We started reading and learning more about the nature of homosexuality. Is it a choice? Is it a lifestyle? Is it a phase? What does the Catholic Church teach regarding homosexuality? Carol sent us numerous books and articles, which we read closely. We noticed more articles and references related to gay issues in newspapers. We kept them out of sight in the house. We would never leave them on a table where friends or neighbors might notice and question why we were reading such material.

We finally ventured into public with our first visit to a support group. It was two months before Christmas—

two months before we would visit Carol and Susan in Phoenix. On a Saturday morning, I called a contact number for the Quad Cities Affirming Diversity organization. I don't remember how I first heard about them, but the number lay on the table for several days before I picked up the phone. A woman answered and when I told her my interest in the meeting, she quickly put her husband on the line. He worked for John Deere and they had a gay son. He gave us the details on where the meeting would be held—at a Unitarian church in Davenport, Iowa, an hour's drive from the farm. We went with our son Kevin and his wife, Darlene. Everyone stood up and talked about their life with a gay family member. When it came time for Joyce and me, it was just too hard. We couldn't do it—we didn't know what to say. We didn't know why we were there. Kevin stepped up and talked for us—for all of us. There were probably fifty people there, and some had true horror stories about what was happening in their family—on some level it started to make our story seem very sane.

Despite finding kindred families at the Quad Cities meetings, after three months, we stopped going—it was just too far to drive from the farm. For the next four years, we basically kept our mouths shut and just went on with our lives. We were thinking about it all the time, but didn't do anything—it just rested as an issue at the side of our family.

I was working as a ski instructor at Sundown Ski Resort, only fifteen miles from our home, and had been for a couple of years by this time. I started skiing when I was sixty-five years old and it was a much younger crowd. Jokes about gays and lesbians were a daily occurrence. I faked a smile but was very uncomfortable and didn't know how to handle the situation. I didn't have the gumption to tell them they shouldn't be telling stories like that. I did not even consider speaking out to try to stop the comments. If I spoke out, people might suspect I had a reason to be soft towards gays.

PART IV

No Turning Back

Chapter Ten

Gays and lesbians create intentional families. There's so much thought that has to go into it. You'll never hear a lesbian woman say she just happened to get pregnant with her partner and decided to keep the baby.

Susan and I talked about having kids for years before we decided to actually do it. I was the one who wanted children. Susan didn't think it was such a good idea, but I had come from a large family and loved the thought of having kids around. It was my idea of a family. We had been together six years when we heard about a six-week class given by an organization named Chrysalis. It was called "Maybe Baby" and was for both gays and lesbians considering having children. We attended the class twice—we needed that double exposure to let all the information soak in and allow our own feelings to bubble to the surface.

Maybe Baby addressed international adoption, domestic adoption, legal issues, medical issues, and the impact on the children themselves of having lesbian and gay parents. A panel of gay and lesbian parents talked about how they had made the decision. These panels were about the logistics: Should it be artificial insemination? If so, how to decide on a donor? Adoption? What was the process for that, and what legal issues might ensue?

Even after going through the sessions twice, we still were undecided. I was pushing for it, but Susan wasn't so sure. Then Susan was ready, and I wasn't sure. We talked about it constantly. Was it fair to children to have them grow up in a family with lesbian parents? Would they be teased? Was it safe for them? Were we being selfish—was it just about us and what we wanted, and were we only pretending to consider the future of the kids as carefully as we were considering our own needs and desires?

There were a lot of angles that were jagged around the edges. We would have to be out—out to everyone—if we decided to be parents. One snowy winter night we were lying in bed under layers of blankets in our Minneapolis home, musing about how we would ever decide. Yes or no. What would ever take us to the point of an actual decision one way or another? Then we started looking at it from a new perspective. We're this far into it. If we have kids, we didn't think we would ever regret it. If we don't, we thought there was a far greater chance of regret. We had finally cut through to our most core feelings. Susan leaned over and said, "Okay, I'm ready."

After that the choices expanded in front of us—we could adopt, we could do artificial insemination, we could have one of us be a surrogate mother impregnated with a fertilized egg from the other. The bottom line became that if the baby couldn't have both of us as biological parents, we at least wanted one of us to be a biological parent. Then there was the decision about the donor. Would it be a known donor? We knew lesbian couples who used the sperm of a male friend. They had to make decisions about how involved the father would be: some chose full involvement, some none at all, and some a world in between. Would the donor be unknown—the sperm of a man who donated to a sperm bank? It was obvious that the known donor was a much more complicated path—now and in the future. Did we want to have the donor come back into the picture later?

We decided to choose an unknown donor. We looked through books of descriptions of donors and analyzed characteristics. We were looking at age, weight, hair color, years of education, nationality, hobbies, and more. Susan joked that we reviewed all the characteristics and information you would learn if you were hanging out with a guy in a bar, but in reality, we knew much more. We analyzed medical histories, education, and nationality, having intense discussions about the impact each of the factors might have on our family or in the city where we lived.

We started charting my temperature every month—like any couple wanting to conceive. Insemination day was on Tax Day, April 15, 1994. The donor had an Irish background—just like both of us. He was outdoors oriented, health conscious. We had pages and pages of medical history. How many straight couples do you know who have an exhaustive listing of medical problems in both their paternal and maternal families, unless they have a serious, known genetic disease? You'd never ask your partner the kinds of questions our donor had been asked.

After the first insemination process, we went on a vacation to Chicago. It was a fatiguing trip with all of the emotional challenges related to the insemination. We couldn't believe we had done it. We went for breakfast, lunch, and dinner with friends and family and toured Chicago.

Back in Minneapolis, we went for pregnancy testing, just to see if it was possible that the insemination had taken. Maybe Baby had prepared us for what could be a long wait. It was typical for couples to take six to nine months before they became pregnant.

The results came back. I was pregnant.

We were stunned and happy. The doctor bragged to her partners in the clinic about getting me pregnant on the first try. Susan summed it up by saying, "Carol's always been an overachiever."

We knew even then we wanted a second child, and the next one would be Susan's biological child. We put away six months' worth of sperm from the same donor, planning ahead.

We'd thought we would have months to prepare our families, including the employees and supervisors at both of our worksites. Neither of us was "out" to anyone at work. I had been at Target since 1991, but my coworkers and supervisor didn't know I had a partner. No one had been to our house. We never had dinner parties where we might be seen as a couple living together, sharing a bedroom. I never talked about Susan as my partner.

We wanted to control the information, not have it whispered that "Carol Curoe is a lesbian and having a baby." Besides the basic information, we also wanted people to know this was a well-thought-out, intentional step. We wanted the people we worked with to understand the seriousness of our decision and how much we had to go through to make this commitment to each other and to a family.

I was prepared to quit my job if it was too hard to be "out" and deal with my coworkers' reactions. I didn't know how it was going to feel. Maybe the work environment would begin to feel negative. The senior vice president of our division had taken such a personal interest in my career to that point, I had to consider the possibility that my forward momentum could slow down or even stop. Things like that are rarely overt. Your work life can just slide into oblivion without anyone ever being able to identify how it happened, what the turning point or beginning of the downward spiral had been.

Susan and I spent hundreds of dollars working with an attorney to anticipate any complications during delivery. Susan needed medical power of attorney in order to direct health care for me and the unborn child. Wills had to be created, and guardianship of the to-be-born child needed to be clearly documented in the event something happened to me during childbirth. It was necessary for me to specify my financial wishes. Our personal commitments or the number of years we had lived together and shared financial resources didn't matter. Nothing would automatically go to Susan unless it was spelled out in the will. We had our lawyer draft a document stating our intentions to coparent this child. It was impossible to legally bind this unborn child to Susan as a parent, but this statement would help if the challenge came up.

Chapter Eleven

Our relative calm was rocked in 1994 when we had another announcement from Carol. Carol and Susan came for a weekend visit and we had a fun time playing cards, golfing, and generally enjoying each other's company. Sunday morning at the breakfast table, Carol spoke up. "Susan and I want to start a family."

Joyce and I were speechless. Wasn't it bad enough to be a lesbian? How could they possibly think it was fair to bring a child into their situation?

"There are definitely a lot of troubled kids out there that need to be adopted," said Joyce.

"Mom, we're not talking about adoption," said Carol. Susan didn't say a word. "We're talking about having our own child, and I'm pregnant already through donor insemination. We were told to plan six to seven months to conceive, and we were going to use that time to help you get used to the idea. Fortunately, or unfortunately, I conceived with our first insemination. The baby is due in January."

I don't think Joyce heard it clearly. Her brain still swirled from the start of the conversation. She kept pursuing the adoption option, floundering with attempts to steer the choices beyond what had been presented as the inevitable. Carol's voice remained steady, constantly bringing the reality of the pregnancy back to the discussion.

I remembered a cold, windy day a few years before when Carol and I were skiing at Deer Valley in Park City, Utah. We were the only two on the chairlift heading to the top of the mountain when Carol told me they were thinking of having a family. I was shocked at the time. I'd never heard of gays having families. I had shelved the information in the back of my mind. I didn't tell Joyce because I secretly hoped it would never come to pass.

"At least if you were adopting a child," said Joyce from another angle, "people might understand you were actually doing something for the good of the community."

"Mom, did you suggest to my siblings they should adopt instead of having a biological child?" Carol said. I could tell she was trying to be empathetic, but continued to make her point.

"I'm guessing that wasn't the case." Carol was in complete control of her emotions and her words. "Susan and I simply want the same thing most couples want. We won't have a child that is biologically both of ours, but at least he or she will be linked to one of us."

I thought it was a mistake. I sat quietly at the table for a while, trying to gather my thoughts and not make a statement I would regret later. Carol and Susan explained their rationale. They had attended a six-week "Maybe Baby" workshop. Twice. There they learned about a multitude of issues associated with lesbians starting a

family: getting pregnant, adoption options, medical issues, legal issues, and telling your family. They explained
that they took the class twice because it was such a difficult decision for them.

They were not "out" in their work lives but knew they
would need to be when they had a family. They were
concerned with how that would be received but confident that if it were required, they could find other employment. They both had graduate degrees and strong
employment histories. Joyce and I were not nearly as
confident. Instead, we could only think of all the difficult challenges that lay ahead of them and this innocent
child.

Carol and Susan drove back to Minneapolis that day,
leaving us to assimilate this new information. Learning
Carol was a lesbian had been a shock. This news eclipsed
that. Sometimes you hear someone say their head was
reeling when confronted with the unexpected. What
does that mean exactly? Now I knew. My head was reeling. The conversation kicked me back to the first letter
when Carol told us she was a lesbian. It was as if we'd
made no progress at all over all of those years.

Later that week, Carol and I spoke on the phone.
"Dad, how are you and Mom doing?"

I really didn't have much to say. Over the next few
days, we'd stabilized, in the same way you stabilize after
an illness, but I really didn't know how we were doing.

We did know from the experience with the first letter
and then learning about homosexuality that we had no

choice but to educate ourselves on this issue, too. Once again, Carol had anticipated us. She wasn't the kind of person, or daughter, to drop a hot issue in our lives and then leave us to grapple with it whatever way we could.

"I've already done a great deal of research," she said. "I'm prepared to give you a wealth of reading material, including numerous articles about children raised by two women, and all of the possible issues: self-esteem, teasing, social adjustment, and legal issues."

"With or without the research," I said, my voice cracking, "I believe this is going to be a mistake, just like buying that tired, run-down 1905 house."

I could have bitten my tongue off. I regret that statement to this day. It was completely out of line—designed to hurt rather than help the conversation. There was silence on the other end of the phone, and then Carol began to cry, sob. She couldn't speak through her tears. The insensitivity of equating having a child to buying a house appalls me still. The phone conversation was cut short after that comment. I had nothing else to say. I never told Joyce what I had said. I was too ashamed.

Over the next days, Carol and Susan made it clear that their intention was to raise this child with two moms and they were prepared to be out. They did not want it to be okay for this child to have two moms in Minneapolis, but not in Iowa. If it was not going to be acceptable to have two moms in Iowa, then they would not be coming to Iowa, and we knew we weren't going to move to Minneapolis. We would lose contact with a loved daughter, and our family holidays and reunions would lack a key ingredient. The hole in our lives would make us all miserable. To treat Carol's lesbianism as a secret was no longer going to work.

Carol and Susan invited Joyce and me to attend the 1994 PFLAG National Conference in San Francisco. With Carol being pregnant, this was probably a good thing for all of us. We wouldn't be alone; Carol and Susan were going, too. Parents and Friends of Lesbians and Gays is a national nonprofit organization with more than 250,000 members. PFLAG's mission is to "promote the health and well-being of gay, lesbian, bisexual and transgender persons, their families and friends through support to cope with an adverse society, education to enlighten all ill-informed public and advocacy to end discrimination and to secure equal civil rights" (www.pflag.org).

The conference was a critical experience in our journey to better understanding the gay and lesbian community and what it had to do with us as parents of a lesbian daughter. It was only a few months until our grandchild would be born, and we needed to prepare ourselves for being open about Susan and Carol. The opening speaker was the father of a lesbian daughter who told us why he spoke out for gay rights and protections. He lived in a very conservative community and faced overt hostility and threats of violence against his family for speaking out. Joyce and I exchanged glances—exactly what we feared ourselves. It was very emotional for everyone there—he spoke to people's worst fears about what could happen to your child or your family. The faces in the audience registered the full range of human emotion. Tears streamed down cheeks. Faces registered outrage or twisted in horror at the stories of what had happened to loved children and friends just because of their sexual orientation.

I was more stoic than many of those seated near me, but inside I had conflicting emotions, too. It was comforting to be with others who understood exactly what we were going through; many also struggled with the Catholic Church's perception of homosexuality. On the other hand, I felt out of my league and even considered the PFLAG conference might be a waste of time and money. These people were taking a public stand for their children and friends. The opening speaker especially had been very courageous. I could not imagine ever being able to do speak out like he did, standing on a stage in front of thousands of people. Nor did I think it would ever be my desire.

There was an added benefit I hadn't anticipated—we got better acquainted with Susan. We were sightseeing, out for a visit to San Francisco, acting like a normal family. One evening we even took a streetcar to the gay district of San Francisco. It was more conventional than Joyce and I expected. Our imaginations had run a bit wild, and I thought I might feel intensely uncomfortable around so many homosexual men and women. You really wouldn't have known the difference between the gays and the others, if you weren't informed. Of course, they were doing all the same things people do everywhere—shopping, going out to dinner, playing with children, talking on their front porch steps. I knew that gays were regular people, but it was good to see it right in front of me.

California was one thing, Iowa was another. Being comfortable on the street in San Francisco didn't take away our anxiety when we got back home. A coworker asked me if I had gone to the "gay" area when we were in San Francisco. I said no, afraid it would be too revealing to say yes. My voice might leak a sympathetic emotion. A warning flag might be raised. Someone might guess I had a reason to go there, might associate it with Carol or another of our children.

When we returned, a couple encouraged us to attend a local PFLAG meeting in Dubuque. By this time, we were doing much better accepting Carol for who she was. I had even subscribed to the *National Catholic Reporter*, a newspaper that can be critical of the Catholic Church, especially around issues of homosexuality. This publication isn't afraid to pick a bone with Rome, so it makes for some provocative reading. It also reassured us that we weren't crazy and that we weren't bad Catholics.

Despite this, we were anxious about the Dubuque meeting. It was two years after we had been to Davenport, but this time it was our own community and it was more risky. We were much more likely to be seen entering the building, be recognized by others, and possibly even know other members. We joined the Dubuque PFLAG chapter that night and still belong in 2007.

We entered the room, not sure what to expect, hoping not to know anyone. People greeted us warmly and I got the feeling they were prepared to help us—they seemed to know we needed help. There were about fifty people at the meeting. It was a large enough group that we should have been able to disappear into the crowd. Then someone shouted out my name (or so it seemed). I wanted to hide, pretend like I hadn't heard—so much for our cover or any secrecy. The woman was a fellow instructor from Sundown Ski School. We had worked together for many years, but neither of us knew the other had a lesbian daughter. We were glad for the camaraderie. People shared the titles of books they had read. We all shared concerns about how society treats homosexuals and the fear that our own children would become targets of hate. We told people we had been to the annual PFLAG conference in San Francisco—we were the only ones who had been there.

Joyce and I still hadn't told anyone that Carol was pregnant. It was clear that time wasn't going to make it any easier.

My first attempt to talk openly about Carol to anyone outside the family was a complete disaster. At the time I had been a business partner with Charles for over ten years in a cattle-feeding venture. I considered him and his wife, Mary Jo, some of our closest friends, and still do. I wanted them to hear about Carol's life from me rather than another source. At that point, it had been four years since we received Carol's first letter.

On a beautiful sunny day in August 1994, Charles, his wife, and I sat at their dinner table sharing lemonade. It had not occurred to me that I might not be ready to talk about Carol's pregnancy. I had practiced my lines on the road to their house like a grade school boy getting ready for the school play.

It didn't go as planned.

Sitting there at the table it occurred to me I was deluding myself. Mary Jo and Charles are devout Catholics, and I imagined they would never be able to accept the story I was trying to tell. After an embarrassing few minutes, as I struggled to get the words out while they looked at me with grave concern, I was able to finally speak.

"Carol is a lesbian." I didn't cry outright, but lost control of my voice and shed tears. "She has a non-Catholic partner, is pregnant, and not married."

Four messages at once—none of which a Catholic father ever dreamed or wished to be telling anyone, even his closest friends. I simply was not able to talk further without breaking down. I kept starting to speak and then would have to stop. I frightened Mary Jo. She reached over and held my hand. They were in complete shock. Empathetic for Joyce and me, though I think they were secretly happy Carol was not their daughter and they were not the ones squeezing this message out to friends over lemonade. They are kind people and said they understood our concerns about religion and thought the Church should be more understanding of homosexuality. After that, it was time to go home. There wasn't much else to say.

It was not much easier a few days later telling Jack, another longtime friend. The two of us sat at his kitchen table drinking coffee. I knew I had to get control of my voice and avoid repeating my experience at Charles's a few days earlier. We grew up in the same area, but I'm quite a bit older than Jack. He had known Carol since she was born. Our kids went to the bank to get their birthday checks cashed and he was the banker.

I looked around at his spotless kitchen trying to find the right words. I drank a lot of coffee with him in that kitchen over the years. Jack hardly got out of the house; he took care of his wife for twenty-two years after she had a stroke. He was her full-time caregiver. He had enough on his plate without listening to my problems.

"Did you know we had a lesbian daughter?"

"No, I did not." Jack's face showed he was stunned.

No small talk or discussion. That was it. He had no firsthand experience with homosexuality and had nothing to say. I was glad I said it. I got his true feelings. That conversation was easier than the one with Charles and his wife—I didn't have to worry about a strict sense of Catholicism guiding Jack's reaction. He's Catholic too, though not as religious as some of our friends. He isn't judgmental and doesn't necessarily use the Catholic Church's doctrine as the filter for his experiences.

With each individual conversation our voices grew stronger, though we had only shared the news with those closest to us. Where this was leading us, we weren't sure.

Our fortieth wedding anniversary was on the horizon, and Joyce and I planned to celebrate with a Mass and reception. The timing was such that Carol would be eight months pregnant. Not something that could be hidden. Carol helped me write a letter that Joyce and I would send to family, friends, and neighbors. Before we mailed it, we decided to talk to our parish priest. We went to his office in Dubuque, not to the church. In retrospect, I'm not sure why we wanted to talk to him. We weren't seeking his permission to send the letter; it was more of a courtesy call because he was a longtime friend of the family. He knew Carol very well and had been in school with our son Kevin.

We were a bit timid, concerned about how he would accept us and our letter. We didn't take it for granted that he would give us his blessing. We had a little small talk when we got there. Joyce was actually too emotionally wrought to talk at all. She cried. He could tell we weren't there just to visit. When we told him Carol was a lesbian and pregnant, he acted completely surprised. He said he hadn't suspected Carol was a lesbian at all.

Looking back, writing the letter was a bold move. It turned out to be one of the best decisions we ever made.

Dear Family and Friends,

We have something we would like to tell you. A letter to relatives and close friends seems to be the best way. It will give you time to think about this and talk to us if you would like.

Four years ago, Carol told us that she is a lesbian and in a committed relationship with her partner, Susan. We were devastated. Why had Carol chosen to be gay? We now realize gays do not choose to be gay anymore than heterosexuals choose to be straight. What they do choose is how to live their lives; one based on integrity or one of denial and hiding. We have found the Church to be more accepting of homosexuals than we once thought.

We have a great deal of love and respect for both Carol and Susan. They live happy and productive lives, and they are active in their church, careers and community.

Carol and Susan have always wanted children, adopted or otherwise. Once again we are faced with many emotions. Carol is now five months pregnant through donor insemination. This decision was not made hastily, but with a great deal of consideration. We, the whole family, will support Carol and Susan in their decision to raise a family. Needless to say, we are worried about the challenges they and this child will have to face in this society, as well as how it might affect their brothers, sisters, spouses and our other grandchildren.

We would like to have your support, but understand that you will have many concerns of your own. Please know that you are welcome to talk them over with us.

Sincerely,
Bob and Joyce

The responses to our letter were overwhelmingly supportive and boosted our confidence. We learned from other parents that a son or daughter was gay. They hadn't come out to the general public, but they told us. We no longer needed to protect our secret or sit silently amid jokes and derogatory comments about gays and lesbians. People no longer made these comments in our presence. The letter also took the fun out of potential gossip. People had no need to whisper, "Did you hear about Carol Curoe?"

We were more at ease than we were before. The many books and articles about homosexuality came out of hiding. After that letter, we wanted people to see them and ask why we had them.

We were enjoying dinner at our house with a priest who celebrated Mass at our church when our regular priest was unavailable. The conversation came around to our family. How were all of the kids doing? How were their jobs and their families? It was time. I asked him if he knew we had a lesbian daughter and he replied simply,

"No, I didn't."

The evening continued. As he was leaving, the three

of us standing on the porch, he paused and asked, "Why didn't you tell me you also had two *heterosexual* daughters?" His meaning was clear to me. He was trying to tell us that he did not see a difference. This question helped open my heart and made it easier to talk to others about Carol.

For the anniversary event, we hired a photographer to take family photos after Mass. He diligently lined everyone up for various shots, just as we had done at other family celebrations for years. While he set up for a photo with our six children and their spouses, he found himself with one extra female—Susan. At first we weren't much help, but we broke out laughing at our daughter Patty's stage-whispered comment, "I guess he didn't get the letter!"

Carol helped him out. "She's with me."

Susan was sent to stand beside Carol for the official family photo.

Chapter Twelve

I helped Mom and Dad write their coming-out letter to their friends and family; it was almost as scary as when we sent our own coming-out letters. In some ways, the stakes felt even higher. This time our fear and anxiety were for those we loved instead of for ourselves. Being in a small rural community, my parents stood to lose a great deal if neighbors chose to turn their backs on them. We joined them in worrying about my siblings and their families. Would the nieces and nephews be teased or ostracized because they had a lesbian aunt? Again, we realized there was no turning back. We couldn't hide this pregnancy, and we sure weren't going to hide a child.

We didn't expect to hear any responses and were very surprised when we started receiving congratulatory cards.

From Dona and Glenn, my sister's in-laws who live on a ranch in South Dakota:

Dear Carol and Susan,

Congratulations on the expectance of a new member to your family. We're very happy for you and know you will be great parents.

I'm sure you're getting many warnings of the hurdles in your chosen path, the stumbling blocks (or should I say hazards and sand traps to golfers?) that will slow you down but these too can be overcome. You are vibrant, caring, loving people with a deep faith and with the support of family and friends you'll make it.

We have a younger friend, who was single, 30 years old and pregnant with a child fathered by a black man, talk about hurdles! She opted to keep the child, stay here and raise her. Fourteen years later she has a very special daughter who has a lot more going for her than many girls the same age from so-called "traditional" home situations.

In this day of so many "alternate" life styles, we accept other people's choices though can't always condone or promote them. We admit we sometimes have trouble understanding them from our side of the spectrum of life but that's our problem and we keep working on it.

We love you and as far as we're concerned you are as special to us as you were before we learned of your lesbian relationship. You have our staunch support.

God Bless you all. We love you.
Dona and Glenn

From my aunt Sister Mary: the front of the card reads "In the freshness of each day . . ." and inside reads "Look for hope in God's love":

Dear Carol and Susan,

Since Robert and Joyce have shared your news, I want to tell you that you have my prayerful support. You have chosen a very difficult path, but you have a great family to support you. The BVM's too, are praying for a "special intention" on the chapel bulletin board. You may have heard of Sr. Mildred who prays for pregnant women, and for infants in need of a good start in life. You will be remembered there, too! You will be in my prayers, too!

Best wishes to both of you!

From my aunt Sister Janita: The front of the card reads "You're on my mind . . ." and the inside reads ". . . and my heart today and every day":

I affirm and support you! I commend you also for your integrity and courage in making your announcement. Hope your family reunion was a relaxing time for all. According to weather reports here, the temperatures were pretty cool!

Love, prayers and best wishes!
Sr. Janita

From a friend and coworker during our Phoenix days, the HR director who gave me the name of a very gay-supportive social worker—even though I never came out to her until we sent her Mom and Dad's letter: The front of the card reads, "C'mon, let's line up." It has a cute picture with a group of penguins with large red letters on their white T-shirts arranged in no particular order. On the inside they are lined up nicely and it spells "CONGRATS ARE IN ORDER!"

Carol and Susan,

This starts a new chapter in your lives. I'm so happy for both of you. This little creature has no idea how lucky he/she will be to have you both as parents. The special challenges ahead will be eased by the love and selflessness you both possess. Yours will be a healthy, love-filled family.

Congrats again!
Much love,
Susan

These cards definitely gave me courage to do what I needed to do at work. First I told my boss. There had been quite a bit of turnover in our department, so when I came into his office, he was sure I was going to tell him I was quitting. That was his big concern. Hearing I was lesbian and going to have a baby was actually a relief. He responded with what often turns out to be the reaction when I tell people I am a lesbian: they tell me they are gay or someone in their family is. For him, it was his brother. We had common ground.

His boss was the senior vice president. He'd been instrumental in my career up to that point, was Catholic, had a big family, and his kids also went to Marquette. We had a lot of shared history, and he kindly and astutely shepherded me through the middle stages of my career. Talking to him was almost as stressful as coming out to my dad. He didn't say much. He listened. I'm sure the fact that I was lesbian had been the farthest thing from his mind.

After him, it was time to talk to the vice president of construction, who had hired me. He'd already retired from Target and was an independent consultant, but I wanted him to hear it from me. My need to tell those who had been my support and mentors came from a base of loyalty, coupled with an anxiety that I was about to reveal potentially career-altering information. There was no way to know if my upwardly mobile career would sustain its momentum after the revelation. Despite my excellent professional track record, would I still be considered a valuable employee? There weren't any role models to affirm or deny this concern. His response was calm and simple: "I respect you for your decision. You're a bright woman and I wish you all the best." We received a very thoughtful card and baby gift from him when the baby was born.

Next, I called my team into the conference room. They were the interior designers and architects who had worked with me for the past two years. I was their boss. They were also afraid I was quitting—they'd had enough chaos with new bosses over the years. I was very nervous. I started the conversation with "I have some personal news that I would like to share with you." My voice cracked. This was the first time I had come out in a public group setting and I was tense. "My partner, Susan, and I have been together for seven years."

They clapped and cheered. I took a deep breath and continued.

"I'm three months pregnant. We're having a baby." They made so much noise with their shouting and laughing that someone came to the door and asked us to be quiet.

By the time of the annual Target Construction Conference, I was eight months pregnant. I geared up for meeting and explaining my life to a whole new set of people who had been my colleagues for a number of years. I was sure the grapevine had already done the initial work for me. The response was a repeat of my revelation at work four months before. I received many supportive and congratulatory hugs. Others came up and excitedly told me they had heard the news. They were filled with questions and blessings for me and my family. I found out, through the ordeal of talking about being a lesbian and pregnant, that everyone has a story to tell. My courage gave them license to tell their own. They shared their revelations with me as if we were all members of a special club—a club where anxiety ran rampant and secrets could make or break your personal relationships and professional life.

We prepared a birth plan documenting our wishes for medical care and also clearly outlining Susan's role as my life partner. The birth plan was shared with all of the midwives. We didn't want to be one of those couples who have an unpleasant surprise in the hospital, when there is a decision to be made and the partner is subtly pushed to the side and not acknowledged as the partner. We made sure there would be no question, no assumption that Susan was just a well-meaning friend hanging out with her pal. She was my partner, the other mother from the start.

We arrived at the hospital at 10:00 P.M. after having watched two sunrises over the course of two long days of labor. During the remainder of labor, we played a game of ditch the nurse. The hospital wanted to force the labor; we were against that strategy. So we "disappeared" around the corner when a nurse was near, took to walking the halls on the sly, willing the labor along. Patrick, who was known as Ziggy the Zygote before we saw his sweet face, was born at 6:00 P.M. the next day without complications, a healthy nine-pound boy. We all slept for ten hours straight, Patrick and Susan in the room with me. The name of our first son alone reinforces the tie to the Catholic Church that continually chafes and reinforces our basic values. There's no name more Catholic, more Irish than Patrick.

In the morning the nurse came into the room and asked how many times I had gotten up during the night to feed the baby. "Feed the baby? None." We'd slept right through what should have been several feedings. Even Patrick knew how exhausted we were.

The day after the birth, I was out of the room and Susan was lying in the hospital bed, still in her pajamas. A new shift nurse arrived to check my stomach. She attempted to examine Susan, not realizing it would be a perfectly flat, smooth stomach. Susan let the moment and the chance for a laugh slide with a clarification: "Two moms here, and I am not the one who just gave birth."

PART V

Mapping Our Way

Chapter Thirteen

Soon after the letter we sent to friends and family at the time of our fortieth wedding anniversary celebration in 1994, we became public advocates for gay rights. I can't say I stood up and shouted, but I became more involved. Joyce and I staffed the PFLAG booths at craft fairs, River Days, and other events in Dubuque. At these events, we sat behind a long table with a PFLAG sign on the front and handed out brochures, pens, and business cards telling when and where monthly meetings were held. The first year, people looked at our table, but few stopped and visited with us. Joyce said later she was glad we didn't see anyone we knew, and she felt guilty about that. No doubt some wouldn't stop because they did not want to be seen visiting with an organization connected to the gay and lesbian community. One time a group of high school students came by and talked to us. They were open to hearing about PFLAG and talked about themselves or kids they knew who they thought were gay. They were bright and curious. Another time, Carol and Susan sat with us. Each year we had more interest and more people ready to visit with us and discuss the issues.

In the years of working at the table, only one person

harassed us. He'd had too much to drink and made some mean comments. His loud voice and swaggering manner got our attention right away. It made us uncomfortable, but we had the right and the obligation to be there. The guy also got the attention of people around us and that of a nearby uniformed police officer. The officer told him to move along, and after a short argument, the man sidled on down the row of tables, probably to berate someone else who was standing up for human rights.

Our increasing awareness that as parents we were the first defense, the primary advocates for Carol and Susan, happened in stages we could handle—one step at a time. I guess we felt that if they had the courage and the energy to take on the challenges, we had better have the courage to stand with them. We grew more confident in telling people about Carol and Susan and their expanding family, and then we were met with the next learning curve: understanding the financial and legal challenges Carol and Susan faced as a lesbian couple with a child.

We attended the Human Rights Campaign (HRC) annual fund-raising dinner and auction in Minneapolis. The HRC is America's largest civil rights organization, and its mission is to achieve gay, lesbian, bisexual, and transgender equality (www.hrc.org). Our eyes were opened as we were introduced to Carol and Susan's friends at this event and heard influential speakers already familiar to us through newspapers and television. Their friends were striking young men and women who were professionals from every type of career, well educated, and well spoken. We were impressed with the size of the group and by the support it received from straight friends, allies, and major corporations.

While the earlier groups we participated in helped us understand homosexuality, realize we were not alone, and cope with this new reality, HRC stretched us in ways we did not anticipate. It challenged us to become more of an advocate for our daughter. It wasn't going to be enough to accept Carol and Susan and hope for their well-being. We became more aware of the real-life issues faced by gays and lesbians in our society. Personal safety was a huge concern. Gays and lesbians were constantly being intimidated and even physically attacked on the streets. They also struggled with legal, financial, employment, and housing barriers that were not an issue for straight people.

Joyce and I learned firsthand of the financial implications Carol and Susan faced when we purchased an investment property with them. Their participation in the venture was much more complicated than ours. Even though they had shared checking and savings accounts for over ten years, they still needed to document Susan's financial contribution in order for her to be recognized as a 25 percent owner in the property. Carol was the one with the cash, since she was working full time, but for tax and estate-planning purposes, they wanted to ensure balanced ownership. As the partnership grew in value with the addition of a second rental property, it was even more difficult for Carol and Susan to maintain balanced ownership. Federal recognition of marriage for same-sex partners would eliminate this complication, one of many benefits not accessible to my daughter and her partner.

Employment security was a whole arena of its own. Carol worked for a fairly progressive corporation that had a policy of nondiscrimination and advocated for diversity among its employees. Many others were not so fortunate and feared being fired or demoted if they came out at work. In the same way you would advocate for any of your relatives who faced discrimination, we were going to have to stand up for Carol and Susan and their friends.

Carol and Susan's friends appreciated our support. They shared many stories with us of gays and lesbians whose coming out created strained family relationships or, worse, severed those relationships. One woman told us how her family basically disintegrated one Christmas Day when her son refused to stay for dinner if his sister's lesbian partner came to the house. We met hundreds of other parents who had journeys similar to ours. Some were in the beginning stages of acceptance; others were farther down that path and were actively advocating for gay rights.

It had been almost six years since we first received Carol's letter telling us she was a lesbian. We were learning and growing and maybe even a little bit proud of how far we had come.

Carol was on the planning committee for the Rainbow Families Conference in Minneapolis for a number of years. Rainbow Families is a regional organization working to build a just, safe, and affirming world for lesbian, gay, bisexual, and transgender parents and their children (www.rainbowfamilies.org). The first year she pulled us in to attend the conference; the second year I helped them set up for the conference; and the third year, she arranged for us to actually present a session. Neither Joyce nor I considered ourselves public speakers, and we were nervous about leading a session and talking about our experience as parents of a lesbian daughter, as grandparents of a child born to lesbian mothers. Carol assured us our personal journey alone made us qualified to present. I prepared a script and planned to read it so that I didn't need to worry about forgetting something or getting off track. Joyce had a few points she wanted to cover and planned to speak spontaneously.

My voice cracked right after I started to speak.

I started and stopped a number of times. The information I was sharing had seemed like old news to me as I prepared it, but speaking about having a lesbian daughter publicly brought up deep emotion. I don't know if I could even describe why—we were too educated at that point to think we were the cause of Carol's lesbianism, so that wasn't it. I think it was just the welling up of how far we had come on this journey. There had been a lot of decisions along the way; it was a constant struggle not to suppress our thoughts and words, or push the feelings down so that we could get on with our lives. Perhaps speaking out was our declaration that we had made it, when in the beginning days, we didn't know if we ever would.

Chapter Fourteen

Political activism was never my forte, but choosing to be an out lesbian with a family made me come forward and advocate for myself, Susan, and our unborn child. Over time, I seemed to find myself speaking on behalf of a broader group.

One policy area that directly affected our family was domestic partner benefits in the workplace. Obtaining such benefits in the workplace was something of a proving ground for lesbians and gays in their quest to be recognized as full functioning members of society. It is an arena in which to stand up and be counted. In 1982, the *Village Voice*, a New York City weekly paper, was the first employer in the United States to offer domestic partner benefits to its lesbian and gay employees. By 1990, there were still fewer than two dozen U.S. employers that offered "spousal equivalent" benefits to their gay employees' partners. But over the next decade, domestic partner benefits in the workplace were added at a rapid pace. According to statistics maintained by the HRC Foundation, the number of employers providing such benefits increased by 18 percent in 2003 alone.

When Patrick was born in 1995, I took six weeks

off from Target for the pregnancy. When I returned, Target had already started discussions within the company about domestic partner benefits, and I now joined in the dialogue. Target's intentions were solid, based on research and the company's determination to be a great workplace for all employees. Target implemented the new benefits, but the process it initially rolled out needed some improvement, so it wasn't a total victory. System requirements didn't allow for an employee to have a domestic partner and legally dependent children on the same plan. If I signed up Susan as my domestic partner, then the children automatically were also classified as domestic partners. Since the government doesn't recognize domestic partners as dependents, any benefits extended to them are taxed as personal income. I would be taxed on the benefits for my biological son; I was not even allowed to provide proof that he *was* my biological son. Adding Susan to my health plan under this scenario did not make financial sense. It was cheaper for us to simply buy our own health insurance policy for her.

I was on the phone with our attorney discussing beneficiaries and casually mentioned the domestic partner insurance issue. She was outraged and urged me to challenge it. I knew Target was aware of the problem and was working to change it. I didn't feel the need to put my career or status on the line for this cause. Target's intentions were good, and as a director for the company, I knew what was involved in implementing those kinds of changes. I was grateful for my job and appreciated the fact that Target had already met the biggest challenge, namely, offering the benefits in the first place.

Following Patrick's birth, we had yet another legal struggle, this time the issue of having Susan adopt Patrick. Same-sex parent adoptions are not guaranteed in Minnesota. Adoptions require court approval, and for same-sex parent adoptions, that approval is at the discretion of the family court judges. When Patrick was born, it was well known that the current presiding judge did not support same-sex parent adoptions. Our attorney recommended that we wait two years before officially applying for Susan to adopt Patrick. At that time, a new judge would be elected and we would have a better chance of getting the adoption approved. We followed her recommendation.

During these years, we updated medical power of attorney documents every six months to ensure Susan's right to provide health care direction for Patrick. We were definitely more confident than Mom and Dad that the next judge would be receptive and would agree to the adoption.

It was a small group at the official ceremony: Susan's parents, Mom and Dad, our attorney, Patrick's godparents, and his nanny. I was surprised at the emotions during the adoption ceremony. The event itself was short, but there were joyful tears and intense feelings of commitment and validation. I'm pretty sure I cried first, but I definitely wasn't the only one! The room flooded with relief, hugging, and congratulations. The judge was wonderful. She was very supportive of us as a family unit and made it clear with her words and actions. As we stood around talking after the ceremony, she addressed Patrick: "I hope I never see you again in my courtroom!" Almost three years old, Patrick was intimidated by the formal atmosphere and the judge's long black robe. He didn't comprehend what it was she wanted him to know, but the adults understood. She didn't want him back in court as a problem juvenile. It was a milestone for us.

The first time Susan and I agreed to speak on behalf of gay and lesbian families was at one of the earlier Rainbow Families conferences. I was on the planning committee, and we needed someone willing to meet with the media. Our second son, Jonathan wasn't born yet, so it was just the three of us. We held Patrick and stood in the bright camera lights while reporters asked us questions. "What is it like to be a two-mom family? What challenges do you face?" We probably disappointed them with our answers. "Well, it's pretty much what every family deals with—managing work and family, sleeping through the night, changing diapers, et cetera."

We called friends to tell them to watch the news. We set the VCR and then waited anxiously to watch ourselves on TV. It was a very short clip, but there we were on a local television station for all to see. I wondered who from Target was watching it and whether I would hear any comments about it Monday at work. It came up in one meeting. A senior vice president asked if it was me that he had seen on the news. I told him it was and the conversation ended there. We were with quite a few people and the meeting was starting, so the fact that it stopped right there didn't seem especially awkward. However, if he was supportive of speaking out, he sure didn't let me know.

When Patrick was born, Susan changed her work schedule to part time. She was working for a consulting firm as an environmental engineer utilizing the master's degree she completed when we moved to Minneapolis. It quickly changed from a career to a job. The projects she was assigned were less challenging and less interesting, but having a baby at home quickly shifted her perspective and the changing work didn't seem like a problem.

We started charting Susan's temperature and were excited about the prospect of adding another baby to our family. A couple of days after our first attempt to impregnate Susan, she came home from work and announced that she had been laid off.

She was upset for about twenty minutes, before reminding herself that she really didn't like the job anyway. Before getting into a serious job search, we decided it would be a nice time for her to be at home with Patrick. She was eligible for unemployment benefits, and I had recently received a promotion, so we felt we could afford it. Knowing that Susan would eventually be back at work, we kept our part-time nanny so that she wouldn't look elsewhere. As time went on, we realized that maybe this arrangement could work for us: Susan staying home with Patrick, and me working full-time. We let our nanny know and gave her plenty of time to find another family.

We still wanted a second child and started thinking seriously about which one of us should be the biological parent. Originally, we planned for it to be Susan so that each of us could experience pregnancy and birth. However, we were already on our own for Susan's health insurance, since she was unemployed. If Susan were the biological mother, we'd need to buy insurance for the baby as well as for her. If I were the biological mother, the baby could be a dependent on my work insurance. After a fair amount of discussion, we decided that I would be the biological mother, which balanced nicely with Susan being the stay-at-home mom and primary caregiver.

Jonathan was two weeks late and a healthy ten-pound baby. The timing was great as Mom and Dad happened to be in Minneapolis for the closing on an apartment building we were purchasing together. They were able to stay home with Patrick while Susan and I went to the hospital with our midwife. Again, it was a very long labor. We managed most of it at home, assuming this delivery was going to be like the first one. As the labor pains became more intense, we waited anxiously for our midwife to come to the house. Being in labor, I had no real sense of time; Susan kept assuring me that not much time had passed, though it seemed like forever since we had called her.

When the midwife finally arrived, we learned that Mom had locked the screen door and there was no way for the midwife to get into the front porch and ring the bell. She eventually found an envelope in her car with which to unlatch the hook. The screen door had not been locked before, and unless Mom was visiting, I don't think it was ever locked again.

Another year at the annual Rainbow Families conference, Mom and Dad were actually presenters. They spoke from the grandparents' perspective. Again, Rainbow Families was looking for a family willing to speak to the media. With Mom and Dad at the conference, we made an interesting choice: a multigenerational family. The interviewer was great at making us feel comfortable. She had us sit at a table in the cafeteria and chatted with us awhile before turning on the cameras. Later, they filmed us walking around the resource fair. Patrick was busy with the children's activities and wasn't included in this interview, but Jonathan was very visible. Again, we called friends to watch the news and set our VCR to record. We waited to see how we did. Overall, we felt like we did a decent job of speaking. However, it's a good thing I am not in the movie or TV business. I can't stand watching myself on the screen.

In 2004, another local television show came to the house to interview the four of us. Rainbow Families often gets calls from the media requesting families for interviews. It's usually very short notice, and the executive director makes a few phone calls to locate someone willing and able to speak. If I'm the one who answers the phone when they call, we're probably more likely to accept the invitation. I've always been more willing to tell our story than Susan, though she has never refused.

We dressed the boys up in their best clothes and explained to them how important it was that they be on best behavior. Like any parents, we wanted our kids to be exemplary!

At the time there was a lot of press around a constitutional amendment proposed by President Bush to ban same-sex marriages. We expected to be part of a well-informed exchange that would cast light on some of the major issues families like ours faced, even in relatively liberal Minneapolis. That illusion was dashed by the first question from the reporter: "Are you married?"

Are we married? We looked at each other with amazement. Of *course*, we're not married—not in the legal sense. You're here to interview us about gay and lesbian rights, and you don't know that gays and lesbians can't be legally married? We were horrified to realize a member of the media was so ignorant about an issue that was so germane to the quality, hopes, and dreams we held for our lives. Patrick was old enough to pick up on the inconsistency, but not necessarily mature enough to be tactful about it. I worried about how he might contradict the reporter. He didn't. He was much more interested in the lights and cameras.

We've spoken on other occasions as well. I was the welcome giver at our church, St. Joan of Arc, one Sunday, a brief address before Mass begins. I used the opportunity to introduce Susan and our two boys and say a bit about how we came to be members of the parish. Joan of Arc is a large congregation, so at least seven hundred people heard about one lesbian family at that Mass. Following the welcome, typically there is an appreciative round of applause for the speaker and everyone stands up for the opening prayers. This morning was no exception. Monday at work, a gay coworker referred to my address. While he wasn't there himself, a friend of his attended the service. His friend was enthusiastically telling him about the wonderful reception this lesbian was given at a Catholic church. My friend knew we belonged to Joan of Arc and made the connection. Not familiar with standard practices of the parish, he assumed the applause and movement were a standing ovation for my mini-speech. I didn't have the heart to tell him that's how our parish responds to all the welcome givers.

We have also spoken frequently at the boys' school. We believe it helps for students and their parents to see us as a family and understand that we really are more like them than different. The first time was with a group of high school students and the upper school chaplain. They have a gay-straight alliance that meets regularly to discuss issues. Jonathan wasn't in school yet, so we took him with us. We were amazed at the confidence and insightful questions that came from this group of teenagers, and left feeling validated in our choice of schools. We have also been invited to each of the boys' classrooms to read about lesbian families. It's interesting that kindergartners and high school students can be equally confident and insightful. It is also an easy reminder that most issues come from the adults, not children.

On other occasions, Mom and Dad have joined Susan and me as we spoke to larger groups of high school students. One night as we were preparing our presentation, I asked Patrick, who was in the fourth grade at the time, "Is there anything you want me to tell them about being in a two-mom family?"

"Tell them it's really hard," he said.

My heart sank. It was exactly what I didn't want to hear, and I was immediately sorry I had asked. "What's hard about it?" I replied, dreading the response.

"Well, lesbian moms are really strict," he said. "They don't let you have Play Stations or watch much TV, and they don't vote for Bush."

Whew! What a relief. At least, I had my opening line for our session!

Patrick has been full of great one-liners over the years. One day he came home from school and told us about a new kid in his class. Most of the students in his class had been with him since preschool, and they all knew he had two moms. This new student didn't.

"He didn't know I had two moms until I told him," Patrick told me.

Taking the high road, I said, "Did he think it was pretty cool?"

"Oh, Mom," he replied. "You sooo overestimate the current public."

Chapter Fifteen

Each of the steps involving recognition of Carol and Susan's relationship and family in the broader legal community opened our eyes, and we usually didn't like what we were seeing. At one point, I began to feel that showing up at PFLAG conferences among the already known supporters of lesbians and gays was not going far enough.

I started a letter-writing campaign.

The only public letter I had ever written in my life was published in the *New York Times* in the 1970s. That was in response to an article disparaging the incentives programs for farmers and displaying ignorance of the hardships farmers go through on an annual basis to get their crops planted, harvested, and sold at market. I never heard from anyone about that. Now, the letters I was compelled to write were of a much more personal nature, and both Joyce and I had a great deal of anxiety about the response. It didn't stop me. It was time.

A well-known high school coach and Boy Scout leader was quoted in the local newspaper: "Young people are not safe in locker rooms or sleeping quarters with gay or lesbian individuals." I was outraged and set out to write a response. I typed it, reading and rereading it for hours, but I also knew I had to get it to the paper fast if I wanted to follow on the heels of the Scout leader's comment and get it printed.

To the Editor of the Telegraph Herald:

> *I wish to commend the* Telegraph Herald *for the editorial in Wednesday's edition which condemned the Dubuque city council for voting down the proposed ordinance that would have prohibited discrimination because of sexual orientation. I am also disappointed with the decision.*
>
> *The* Cedar Rapids Gazette *also ran a story on this council meeting on Wednesday. According to that article, a local football coach and Boy Scout leader was quoted as saying that people applying for positions in which they supervise young people's locker rooms and sleeping quarters should be asked about their sexual orientation. "Otherwise it would be like a fox guarding the hen house."*
>
> *As the father of a lesbian daughter, I am deeply offended by his remarks. Saying young people are not safe in locker rooms or sleeping quarters with gays or lesbians quite clearly demonstrates a lack of education on this issue.*
>
> *Bob Curoe*

You have permission to print this, but not permission to alter or delete parts without my consent. If you use this letter I would request that you not print my phone number. Thank you.

I was nervous about sending this signed letter, afraid what people would think and say. It took me back to my initial fears about public exposure and outrage—aimed at me or my family. I was now exposed to the whole community. My name was at the bottom. Anyone who wanted to could respond in writing to the paper, drive to my home and knock on my door, call me on the phone, or hurl a stone through my window.

The morning the paper was printed, I received three e-mails. They complimented me on my message and supported what I had written. Joyce and I went out for a while. When we returned there was a different kind of message on the answering machine. It was from a man who had recently moved from Chicago to Dubuque. His tone was belligerent. I assumed he was sober—it was only 8:30 in the morning when he left the message, though being drunk might have explained his rudeness. We stared at the phone listening to his angry voice. He disagreed with me and had no hesitation in saying it. He left his name, address, phone number, and his frank opinions and asked me to call him.

Joyce was afraid. She had a vivid imagination and she let it go wild with what this man might do. I have to admit it was disturbing—a voice like that right in your own home. I did not return the call and I never heard from him again.

Having the guts to send that letter to the editor took the fear out of people learning about our story. Speaking out became easier. I no longer held back my thoughts or words when someone told jokes about gays or lesbians. Instead, I told them they should be careful telling jokes of that type because it might be offensive to people. My advice shut people right up. I only had to say it once. After that they never made those kinds of comments again.

I took courage from other people who stood up for their rights and those of their colleagues and families. In 1999, Bill Bradley campaigned for the Democratic Party's nomination for president of the United States. He reportedly gave a stirring talk at the Human Rights Campaign at Dearborn, Michigan, about civil rights in general and gay rights in particular. Over the years, I have read and reread a story Bradley told that evening: In late 1946, General Eisenhower called Sergeant Johnnie Phelps (a woman) into his office and said that he had heard there were lesbians in the headquarters WAC battalion. He wanted her to compile the women's names so that he could get rid of them. Phelps responded that discharging members from one of the most decorated units in service would have serious consequences on the labor pool. She concluded her remarks by saying, "I will make your list, but you need to know that when the list comes back, my name is going to be first." Eisenhower's secretary, also in the room, corrected Sergeant Phelps: "Sir," she injected, "the sergeant's name will be second. I am going to type the list. My name will be first." Eisenhower looked at her, looked at the sergeant, shook his head, and said, "Forget the order. Just forget about it."

That same evening, Bradley also quoted President Harry Truman. Being a longtime supporter and admirer of Truman's, I found his message extremely hopeful. "I believe in the Constitution and the Declaration of Independence. If you do that also, then everybody has got to have their rights and that means everybody. It doesn't matter a damn bit who they are."

My next letter to the editor was printed in the *Des Moines Register*. It was in response to a column published on April 20, 2003, Easter Sunday.

> *I wish to commend Rekha Basu on her April 20th column. It was in response to the radio talk show host Jan Mickelson and his opinion on the Roosevelt High School Straight and Gay Alliance. Basu said, "It's gone beyond ignorant and offensive to downright creepy." It showed ignorance in that Mr. Mickelson did not have his facts straight; it was offensive to many, both straight and gay; and it is creepy that in a time of war and terrorism, he has chosen to attack a group of high school students.*
>
> *The prejudice and intolerance shown by Mickelson are a clear demonstration of why these organizations are needed to keep our youth safe.*

As the father of a lesbian daughter, I am person-
ally insulted and frightened by Mr. Mickelson's cruelty.
His bigotry flames the fires of intolerance and fosters
hate crimes like that which killed Matthew Shepard
in Wyoming. It also allows individuals to feel justified
in discriminating against gays and lesbians in employ-
ment and housing.

I would also like to commend Roosevelt High School.
The comments made by their Principal, Anita Micich
and their Counselor, Al Foote, show recognition of the
need to protect and support all students. The Straight
and Gay Alliance was formed to promote tolerance and
prevent discrimination against all students, regardless
of sexual orientation. The prejudice and intolerance
shown by Mr. Mickelson have, as Rekha said, "put a
face on the hatred they were trying to expose."

I would question the judgment of the radio station
to air such a program. Would it allow this if it was
directed at other minorities such as religious or racial
minorities?

Bob Curoe

By spring 2004, my letter-writing focus had expanded
to audiences beyond our local community.

Dear Senator,

I was surprised and disappointed to read in the
March 25th issue of the Telegraph Herald *that you*

voted for the State constitutional amendment requiring marriage to be between a man and a woman. I was surprised because I believe the amendment is mean-spirited and I didn't expect that from you. I was disappointed because I supported your election and now feel I have made a mistake.

I realize the majority of your constituents in this district are conservative and that you may be trying to represent that majority. However, history has shown that the majority are not always correct. Over a hundred years ago, the majority of people in the United States were against the freedom of slaves. As recently as the 1960s, the majority of people in the United States were also against making inter-racial marriages legal. If elected officials of our past did what the majority wanted instead of what was right, our country would be a very different place today.

"Equal rights" means equal rights for all. The founding fathers of our constitution designed our constitution to protect the civil rights of all individuals, not to take rights away. As Equality magazine states in the spring 2004 issue: "We must demonstrate that standing up for equality and against discrimination is a winning formula."

As for the argument of protecting the institution of marriage, there must be better ways to "protect" marriage than to amend the Constitution. With over 50% of our marriages ending in divorce courts, efforts focused on keeping marriages together would seem more productive than keeping committed individuals from joining in the institution.

Obviously, as the father of a lesbian daughter, I have strong feelings on this issue which are contrary to yours. As a result, I will be unable to support you in your re-election by allowing your signs on our yard this summer and fall.

Sincerely,
Bob Curoe

I find it very encouraging when families like my daughter's are reflected positively side by side with a "typical" family structure. A series of stories in the *Des Moines Register* included a two-mom family. I thought it was great, but a schoolteacher from the region disagreed with the inclusion. Once again, I felt compelled to speak out.

Dear Editor:

I am writing in response to the editorials from Becky Simpson and Arlene Cook regarding "The Daily Struggle" stories in last week's Register.

As the father of a lesbian daughter, I was happy to see the Baird family included, even though, as Arlene Cook indicated, they do not reflect a "broad range of typical." My daughter is in a committed relationship with her partner of seventeen years and together they are raising two children. I found it refreshing that the

Register *reflected my family as well as the diversity of its readers.*

Arlene Cook, a teacher, also indicated she is not a "Lesbophobe." I could not find this word in the dictionary, so I can only assume she is not. However, I can say with confidence that I am happy my grandchildren are not in her classroom learning her definition of a "typical family."

Sincerely,
Bob Curoe

PART VI

Picking Up Speed

Chapter Sixteen

Although I was raised Catholic and had seventeen years of Catholic education, you'd be hard-pressed to call me a "good" Catholic or maybe even "a Catholic." We belong to a Catholic parish and I go to church; in my heart, that doesn't make me a Catholic. There's so much about the Church that I don't agree with, and I'm always battling its policies in my mind. I like our parish. I rationalize that we belong to St. Joan of Arc parish, not the larger Catholic Church.

When I was growing up, I don't remember knowing anyone who wasn't Catholic. The neighbors were Irish or German Catholics, but all Catholics. I don't remember any Jews, Lutherans, or anyone from any other religion. Being Catholic was the reference point for our lives. Even when it would have been easy to skip Mass and lie about it when we were in high school, we still went to Mass every weekend. It was easier than dealing with the guilt.

I like a lot about St. Joan's. Our church's mission statement is, *We welcome you wherever you are on your journey.* We value thinking and speaking out, analyzing the issues,

coming to our own thoughtful conclusions without whole-
sale acceptance, or dismissal, of the doctrines and policies of the Church. The first time Susan and I attended
St. Joan of Arc, a lesbian rabbi spoke. She was great, ad-
dressing the need to focus on our similarities instead of
our differences. In any one month, we might hear from
people speaking out against the war or advocating for
the rights of the mentally ill, showing photos sent by
church delegations visiting Africa, or representing a nonprofit for the homeless.

The youth activities are a big part of our church and
expand beyond traditional religious education. The programs range from sports like bowling, skiing, and snow-
tubing to community service activities in which a group
prepares meals for homeless persons. Kids anywhere
from three years old through high school age attend.
Our director of elementary religious education is a lesbian with a number of adopted children. She has such
an exciting, welcoming program that she won an award
from the archdiocese. Later, the archdiocese withdrew
the award, causing pandemonium in our parish. A reli-
gious-right group apparently started an e-mail campaign
to the Archdiocese of St. Paul and Minneapolis asking for
withdrawal of the award because she was a lesbian. I was
moved by the actions of the parish, both straight and gay.
The parish held a number of sessions with prayerful dialogue to discern how to respond. I joined approximately
fifty men, women, and children to peacefully protest and
sing outside the awards ceremony. I had never stood in

any kind of protest, and I was moved by the passion and support of church staff and straight members of the parish. The approach was not angry or aggressive, but it wasn't just ignoring the situation either.

Bishop Thomas Gumbleton of Detroit has been a strong advocate for victims abused by Catholic priests, as well as for gays and lesbians. Bishop Gumbleton was the longest-serving bishop in the United States when his request to remain active instead of retiring at the mandatory age of seventy-five was denied in 2006. He holds numerous Honorary Doctorate of Education degrees from institutions across the country and has received dozens of awards for his activism. Bishop Gumbleton is known for his focus on the message and strategies of world peace. He became politicized on the topic of homosexuality after receiving a letter from his own brother, who told him he was gay. After this personal experience, he began to speak out on the need for the Catholic Church to take an informed and intelligent view on gays and lesbians. He advocates for homosexual clergy being truthful to themselves and others—to have the courage to stand up and speak out.

Bishop Gumbleton was relieved of his duties as pastor of St. Leo Parish in Detroit in February 2007. Shortly before, he was forbidden to speak in Tucson, Arizona, when invited by the local Call to Action (CTA) chapter, an organization of Catholics dedicated to scrutinizing church policies and working for social justice in the world. CTA has its roots in the 1976 Call to Action conference, which was organized and planned by the U.S. Catholic bishops. The following editorial in the *National Catholic Reporter* (February 9, 2007) refers to this incident:

> Our hunch, for what it's worth, is that [the local] Call to Action [chapter] in this instance provided Tucson Bishop Gerald F. Kicanas the cover he needed so that he could avoid directly dealing with Gumbleton and the topic of his talk: "Homosexuality and the Church." That last point, of course, is a matter of ecclesial politics, which one can choose to engage or ignore. We advise the latter.
>
> What's important in all of this is how it was resolved. The Tucson chapter of Call to Action, which claims a mailing list of about 150 people, found a local Disciples of Christ Church willing to host the good bishop. And so, Catholics who want to hear what Gumbleton has to say will get a "two-fer" for their efforts—a good talk (it's been our experience that Gumbleton presents a balanced, thoughtful and prayerful consideration of difficult issues) and a dollop of ecumenical goodwill. Not a bad evening.
>
> The lesson to take away is significant and important to understand, if simple. Adult Catholics need not ask permission or seek approval to have a simple conversation or to call upon respected and credible thinkers who may not find favor with the local hierarchy. . . .
>
> We can all do this to one degree or another. It doesn't require fighting with anyone or disparaging anyone.

Lots of other speakers come through our dioceses, too, who won't rile the bishops and also have important things to say. They should be supported. Ignore those you think not worth your time. It's a mature way to express your faith.

There's just no reason to be limited or anxiety-ridden.

Adult, educated Catholics need not allow their faith or their Catholic identity or their intellectual curiosity to be defined solely by a parish building, diocesan programs or the whims of a bishop. We can do what we need to do.

Ironically, a breakfast with the controversial Bishop Gumbleton, Susan, and Dad was the most real the Catholic Church has ever been for me. Unfortunately, Mom wasn't able to join us; she would have really enjoyed it. Bishop Gumbleton spoke at the Basilica in Minneapolis and we invited him to have breakfast with us while he was in town. I was both inspired and surprised; he is a man of small stature, soft spoken, and confident. He speaks with integrity and without vindictiveness toward the Church, despite the way he has been treated. I was moved by his passion and commitment for working within the Church to change what he thinks needs to be changed.

Susan and I struggled to decide whether we wanted to baptize Patrick, and any future children, into the Catholic Church. We wanted to baptize him into our parish, but felt that baptizing him into the larger Catholic Church was hypocritical. My parents were distraught over our need to wait until we felt sure about what to do, to make a decision that was consistent with our values and beliefs. Mom and Dad were patient, but I knew it was very important to them.

It took many months for us to make the final decision to do it. A decade later we can laugh about it, saying Patrick was the only boy in that group who walked to his own baptism. Our church has a committee that decorates baptismal garments. The usual cross-stitching on the traditional stole is lovely and features such Catholic motifs as the cross, set out in white silk threads. For Patrick, the committee embroidered not only the cross but also a rainbow, the universal symbol of light, hope, and the unity of gays and lesbians everywhere.

Susan and I don't pretend to be anything we aren't in terms of the Church. We've made it clear to our sons that the majority of leaders of the Catholic Church do not think homosexuality is okay—in fact, they routinely disparage it and couch it in pretty ugly terminology. We do not protect our sons from the knowledge that many people and organizations not only may not agree with having two lesbians for parents—in fact, they may actively work against it.

And the Catholic Church isn't the only organization that takes this stand. We cringed the day a request to join Cub Scouts came home from school with Patrick in first grade. The Cub Scouts' parent organization, Boy

Scouts, while sponsoring a plethora of fun and stimulat-
ing activities for boys and young men, also asserts that
"homosexual conduct is inconsistent with the values" it
seeks to instill, "particularly with the values represented
by the terms 'morally straight' and 'clean'" (*Boy Scouts of
America and Monmouth Council et al. v. James Dale*; the U.S.
Supreme Court handed down a ruling agreeing with the
Boy Scouts on June 28, 2000). It was hard to imagine our
son going to a club every week that actually had taken
a stand declaring our life to be inappropriate and even
immoral. We talked about it at the dinner table. "Patrick,
you can definitely join, but we want you to know that the
people at the top don't think it is okay to be a two-mom
family." He easily processed this information and decided that he didn't want to join. Instead, he was going
to set up his own club, one that didn't discriminate. He
wanted to call it "Rainbow Scouts." Later, when close
friends joined the Boy Scouts in fifth grade, Patrick was
surprised and somewhat offended. We pointed out that
just because people join an organization, it doesn't mean
they agree with everything it stands for; our member-
ship at St. Joan of Arc was a simple analogy. We were
also able to point out that he had both an uncle and a
cousin who had achieved the high honor of being an
Eagle Scout.

Chapter Seventeen

It has been seventeen years since we got that first letter from Carol telling us she is a lesbian. It was just the beginning of our struggle to know how we could support our daughter and also follow the teachings of the Catholic Church. The issue is difficult for me to understand and harder yet to put into words. Prior to Carol sharing with us that she is a lesbian, Joyce and I did not give the Catholic Church's view on homosexuality much thought. It did not directly impact us.

Once Carol came out to us, the internal struggle became quickly apparent. We were firm in our belief that we would never turn our back on our daughter, but disappointed as we reached out for support from the Catholic Church. We understand that a number of Catholic clergy also disagree with Rome on this issue. That doesn't necessarily provide much relief. I am not an expert on the Bible, but individuals seem able to find any interpretation in it they want.

Now we have concerns that go beyond our daughter. Joyce and I think about our grandsons and their relationship to the Catholic Church. When Carol and Susan struggled with the decision to have Patrick and Jonathan baptized, we struggled with them. It pained us to think our grandsons might not be baptized in the religion that had been our anchor our entire lives. Baptism is the first Sacrament in the Catholic Church, and we view it as a critical link in the chain of important events for a Catholic child.

We had no choice but to try to understand Carol and Susan's dilemma. They struggled with what seemed hypocritical: having the boys baptized in their local parish, which accepted and affirmed them, but realizing that technically it also meant baptizing them into the larger Catholic Church, which did not accept them.

In the end, after much discussion, they came to the decision to have the boys baptized, and it is recognized as a true baptism in the Catholic Church. I hope the boys can proceed with the Sacraments regardless of how the Church feels about homosexuality. Confirmation will be the next important Sacrament for them—the next step. We hope that since the Church recognized their baptisms, their confirmations can easily follow. Joyce put it best when one night she said to me, "I hate to think about the possibility that the boys will not receive the other Sacraments. But I'm not looking for trouble. I hope it will turn out different than my fears."

To gain understanding and become more accepting of the Church's views, we tried to become educated about the various perspectives on the Catholic Church and homosexuality. Our research on the history of homosexuality and the Catholic Church has both informed and confused our own journey to come to peace with who our daughter is.

One beacon of hope we saw in the Catholic Church's stand on homosexuality came in 1997, with the American Catholic bishops' pastoral letter "Always Our Children," which emphasized the importance of unconditional love for our children, whatever their sexual orientation. This compassionate letter was a call to parents and others to see gays and lesbians as gifted persons who are equal members of their Christian communities. It gave us much hope as it directly addressed one of our deepest fears: that we would be abandoned by the Church as we worked through our own feelings about Carol. We would be alone. "Always Our Children" directly refuted this fear:

> *You need not face this painful time alone, without human assistance or God's grace. The Church can be an instrument of both help and healing. This is why we bishops, as pastors and teachers, write to you.*

In 1976, Jesuit Father John J. McNeill published *The Church and the Homosexual*, a thoughtful discussion of the way the scriptures address homosexuality, and the book received a great deal of attention from the Catholic community. He was the first Catholic theologian to openly challenge the Church's teachings on homosexuality. In

1987, Father McNeill left the Jesuit order, and he has spent the rest of his life continuing to help gay men and women.

In 2000, Joyce and I attended an all-day workshop in Iowa City conducted by Sister Jeannine Gramick. She told of her work with Father Bob Nugent, their growing international following, and their long struggle with the Vatican. Father Nugent is a member of the Salvatorian order and Sister Jeannine originally belonged to the School Sisters of Notre Dame. In 1977, they founded New Ways Ministry in Mount Rainer, Maryland, for Catholic gay and lesbian people. They traveled widely giving talks and workshops about the reconciliation of Catholicism and homosexuality. While receiving their message twenty years later was a breath of fresh air for Joyce and me, the Vatican had opposed their work.

On July 14, 1999, Father Nugent and Sister Jeannine received notification from the Vatican, signed by Cardinal Joseph Ratzinger (now Pope Benedict XVI), that they were banned from continuing their ministry to homosexuals, similar to what happened to Father McNeill when he spoke out. They were told that their message did not follow Catholic doctrine closely enough, namely, that "homosexual acts were intrinsically disordered and the homosexual orientation was objectively disordered." For Catholics, short of excommunication from the Catholic Church itself, being silenced by the Vatican is the most alarming and traumatic thing that can happen to you. A dictate from the Holy See is a signal to your peers and family that you have crossed a line and are following a dangerous path.

On May 23, 2000, a second and more extensive order was delivered by their Superiors General who ordered them to not speak pubicly about homosexuality. Nugent eventually accepted the Vatican's direction and returned to parish ministry as a priest in good standing. Sister Jeannine refused to stop her ministry to homosexuals. According to New Ways' Web site, she transferred to the Sisters of Loretto in 2001 because they supported her ministry. At the workshop Joyce and I attended in Iowa City, Sister Jeannine asked each one of us in the crowd of about 150 to write to their archbishop requesting that he appeal to the Vatican to rescind the order for her to stop her work. I did write to our archbishop. He responded but refused to get involved.

In recent years, the Catholic Church appears to be stiffening its stance on homosexuality. In November 2005, the Vatican issued a statement regarding the ordination of gay priests, appearing to rebut the earlier "Always Our Children" pastoral letter, which was intended to be an outstretched hand to gays. The Vatican's document stated:

> [E]ven while deeply respecting the persons in question, [we] cannot admit to Seminary or Holy Orders those who are actively homosexual, have deep-seated homosexual tendencies, or support the so-called gay culture. Such people, in fact, find themselves in a situation

that seriously obstructs them from properly relating to men and women. The negative consequences that can result from the Ordination of persons with deep-seated homosexual tendencies should not be obscured.

In meetings with the candidate, the spiritual director must clearly recall the Church's demands regarding priestly chastity and the specific affective maturity of the priest, as well as help him discern if he has the necessary qualities. He has the obligation to evaluate all the qualities of the personality and assure that the candidate does not have sexual disorders that are incompatible with priesthood. If a candidate is actively homosexual or shows deep-seated homosexual tendencies, his spiritual director, as well as his confessor, has the duty to dissuade him, in conscience, from proceeding towards Ordination.

In my opinion, the Vatican's position is uncharitable and condemning; as such, it is hard to accept and understand. To hear the Catholic Church make such statements is frustrating and challenges our core religious beliefs.

We have, however, found reason for cautious optimism in small places. In February 2005, the Dubuque Human Rights Commission attempted to get sexual orientation added to that city's human rights ordinance. This became a controversial issue and numerous letters were published in the paper. A Catholic priest, Father

Thomas Rhomberg, wrote the following letter to the editor on the Catholic view of the homosexuality:

> *The proposal by the Dubuque Human Rights Commission to include sexual orientation as another class of people who would be protected from unjust discrimination seems misunderstood by some fellow Catholics. This ordinance and my support of it are not about homosexual acts, or about support or approval of them. It is about our treatment of homosexuals.*
>
> *The Catechism of the Catholic Church states, and I quote: "Homosexuals must be accepted with respect, compassion and sensitivity. Every sign of unjust discrimination in their regard should be avoided." (Par. 2358 on page 566).*
>
> *Our Catholic bishops said: "Homosexual persons, like everyone else, should not suffer from prejudice against their basic rights, (food, clothing, housing, health care, education, security, social services and employment). They have a right to respect, friendship and justice. They should have an active role in the Christian community." (Human Sexuality, par. 55; To Live in Christ Jesus, par. 52).*
>
> *Jesus, in sharing meals with "sinners," was not supporting or approving their lifestyle, but revealing the unconditional and all-inclusive love of God. Jesus was often misunderstood and criticized for associating with those who seemed to be outside the circle of approval,*

by those who took it upon themselves to judge who was worthy or unworthy of God's love.

In light of the teaching of Jesus by his word and example, supporting this amendment to the city ordinance that would include "sexual orientation" as a protected class against discrimination is exactly what we are instructed to do by the Catechism of the Catholic Church.

There is no easy solution to the reconciliation between the Catholic Church and the issue of homosexuality, but I feel nationally syndicated columnist Donald Kaul summarized it well. He wrote about the Bible and homosexuality as it related to a school board election in Des Moines, where a gay man was running for a position on the school board:

One of the arguments against teaching homosexuality in schools is that the Bible says it is evil. That has to be flat out wrong. God must have been distracted by a falling sparrow or something when he wrote that. Either that or it's a typographical error. Homosexuality is not evil: it is not virtuous: it merely is. I am sure God will correct the error when he gets around to the second edition.

This article gave me hope and I kept it.

Chapter Eighteen

I am also hopeful about the future when I see the insight and understanding that is present in the next generation. They can carry on the work that needs to be done to create a world safe for everyone. I see the possibility in a college application essay written by one of my grandsons:

Seated around the table are four people from different backgrounds, with different opinions. The scenario: a card game. The discussion: politics. My partner for the game is my grandfather, who has lived through fourteen presidents, the Great Depression, and raising six kids. Playing against us are two of my aunts. One aunt's parents emigrated from communist Cuba and the other aunt is a lesbian who lives happily with her life partner and two boys.

My aunt from Cuba is perhaps one of the most passionate people I know. She is Hispanic and this heritage plays an important role in her life and shaping her views. Her family fled a dictatorship to come to a country that accepts and supports diversity. Her faith in the freedom of ideas and the tolerance of diversity

and the sacrifices her family has made in pursuit of
this freedom make me appreciate how fortunate I am.

As the parents of two boys, my other aunt Carol and
her partner Susan are one of the first families that come
to mind when I think of a loving family. Carol teaches
me that perseverance and individuality can rise above
adversity.

Accepting of these two women is my grandfather,
a 79-year-old Irish-Catholic farmer, born and raised in
Iowa. Of the three, his lesson has the most impact on
me. He has learned to accept a number of unexpected
twists and turns presented to him by his children, many
challenging his Catholic beliefs. Rather than meet each
situation with close-mindedness, my grandfather took
each new obstacle in stride and started a personal mission of acceptance and understanding.

With such a range of backgrounds and opinions, the
discussion around the card table is expectedly heated.
However, the game continues, partners remain partners, and laughter prevails over tears. The card game
and its players show me that the unifying qualities that
connect us are the important qualities, not the dividing
ones.

My hope is that no child or adult in the future needs
to fear the realization that they are gay —that they could
be supported by their families, friends and neighbors,
and faith communities, and know they had a safe haven
in which to live their life.

Conclusion

It's been almost seventeen years since I came out to my parents. If we didn't have the letters to remind us, it might be easy to forget how difficult it was in the beginning. There have been a lot of tears, fears, questioning, and even anger. We have grieved for the person we thought I was, letting go of old dreams and replacing them with new ones. It's been a journey none of us anticipated, but we are all richer because of it.

Our lives today are much more similar to than different from those of our friends with children of similar ages. We hope the boys are learning and enjoying school; we're planning for their college and saving for our retirement. We struggle to balance work, family time, and time as a couple. We want a future for our sons that is rich with love, friendships, health, and prosperity.

We also want a future for gays, lesbians, and their families that is free from discrimination, hatred, and ridicule. By sharing our story, we hope it might give other families strength to tell their stories, too. With our combined voices, we can be heard clearly, causing future generations to wonder why a book like this ever needed to be written.

Resources

**Catholic Rainbow Parents
(www.cpcsm.org/catholicrainbowparents.htm)**
Organization of Catholic parents working for reformation within the Church—as well as within society—by speaking their own truth, as the most qualified experts, about their GLBT children and their children's lives.

COLAGE (www.colage.org)
Children of Lesbians and Gays Everywhere works to engage, connect, and empower people to make the world a better place for children of lesbian, gay, bisexual, and/or transgender parents and families.

Dignity (www.dignityusa.org)
DignityUSA works for respect and justice for all gay, lesbian, bisexual, and transgender persons in the Catholic Church and the world through education, advocacy and support.

Family Pride (www.familypride.org)
Family Pride is a national nonprofit organization committed to securing family equality for lesbian, gay, bisexual,
transgender and queer parents, guardians and allies.

GLSEN (www.glsen.org)
Gay Lesbian and Straight Education Network is a national organization paying attention to homophobia in
schools. Chapters are located throughout the country.

HRC (www.hrc.org)
The Human Rights Campaign is America's largest civil
rights organization working to achieve gay, lesbian, bisexual, and transgender equality. By inspiring and engag-
ing all Americans, HRC strives to end discrimination
against GLBT citizens and realize a nation that achieves
fundamental fairness and equality for all.

**The Matthew Shepard Foundation
(www.matthewshepard.org)**
Matthew Shepard was murdered in an anti-gay hate crime
in Wyoming in October 1998. The Matthew Shepard
Foundation seeks to "Replace Hate with Understanding,
Compassion & Acceptance" through its varied educa-
tional, outreach, and advocacy programs and by continuing to tell Matthew's story.

New Ways Ministry (mysite.verizon.net/~vze43yrc)
New Ways Ministry provides a gay-positive ministry of advocacy and justice for lesbian and gay Catholics and reconciliation within the larger Christian and civil communities.

PFLAG (www.pflag.org)
Parents, Family and Friends of Lesbians and Gays works to promote the health and well-being of gay, lesbian, bisexual, and transgender persons, their families and friends through: support, education, and advocacy to end discrimination and to secure equal civil rights.

Rainbow Families (www.rainbowfamilies.org)
Rainbow Families works to build a safe, just, and affirming world for lesbian, gay, bisexual, and transgender parents and their children.

Book Group Discussion Topics

1. How do you think Bob and Carol's experience compares to that of other parents and children in similar situations?

2. How do you think your son or daughter would deal with the revelation that he or she is gay? How do you imagine you would respond?

3. What comments have you heard about gays and lesbians? How did you respond?

4. How do you think you would respond if your son or daughter wanted to visit a friend who has two moms or two dads?

5. What policies and procedures does your children's school have in place to prevent and address bullying and abuse of students and faculty who are different?

6. How do you feel about a constitutional amendment that limits marriage to a man and a woman only?

7. How do you think Carol and her partner experienced discrimination? What can be done about it?

8. Compare Bob's and Carol's coming-out stories.

9. How did Bob and Joyce's faith conflict with their love for their daughter?

10. How do other religions view homosexuality?

Carol and Bob would be willing to meet with your book group if time and location can be accommodated.

About the Authors

Robert Curoe lives in eastern Iowa, where he and his wife, Joyce, grew up and raised their six children. Robert farmed a grain and livestock operation and taught downhill skiing until he retired at the young age of eighty-one.

Carol Curoe is a business consultant in Minneapolis, where she lives with Susan, her partner of almost twenty years, their sons, Patrick and Jonathan, and dog, Max. Carol has a B.S. in civil engineering from Marquette University, a master's in international management from Thunderbird School of Global Management, and a certificate in organizational development from the University of St. Thomas.